AYRSHIRE MONOGRAPHS 26

Servants in Ayrshire

1750–1914

Jean Aitchison

D1437519

Published by

Ayrshire Archaeological and Natural History Society

Ayr, 2001

Printed by

The Cromwell Press, Trowbridge, Wiltshire

Since retiring from teaching in Ayrshire, Jean Aitchison has pursued an interest in Scottish history, culminating in this monograph which is an edited version of the work undertaken for the degree of M.Phil. awarded by the University of Glasgow.

Copyright © 2001 by Jean Aitchison

cover design by David McClure

edited and typeset for the AANHS by
Rob Close, Bill Layhe, David McClure and Stanley Sarsfield

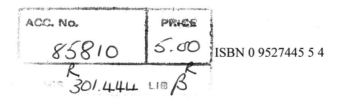
ISBN 0 9527445 5 4

Contents

List of Illustrations 4

Acknowledgements 5

Introduction 6

Chapter 1: The Master–Servant Relationship 11

The master–servant relationship as defined in law 11

The master–servant relationship as recommended by the Church 18

The master–servant relationship in practice 22

Chapter 2: Hiring and Firing 28

Finding a Place by Word of Mouth 28

Feeing Fairs..30

Employment Agencies...36

Newspaper Advertisements 41

Termination of Employment 43

Chapter 3: Conditions of Service 47

Wages, Hours and Duties 47

Accommodation 52

Food and Drink 56

Clothing..59

Chapter 4: Population Changes 73

Migration to another place of service 73

Emigration..76

Chapter 5: The Concerns of Everyday Life 81

Health Care, Retirement and Death...81

Savings and Insurance...85

Poverty 91

Crime and Punishment 95

Leisure and Literacy..100

Postscript..110

Appendix 1: Kirkdandie Fair...112

Appendix 2: Employment Agencies 113

Appendix 3: Female Friendly Society Rules and Regulations............115

Appendix 4: Tables of Wages and Prices...120

Appendix 5: Servant Tax Returns...128

Index...134

List of Illustrations

Illus. 1: Map of the County of Ayr, Sayer & Bennett, November 1777...................8

Illus. 2: Cunninghame...9

Illus. 3: Kyle. 9

Illus. 4: Carrick. 10

Illus. 5: Extracts from Ayr Burgh Register of Incarcerations, Liberations and Arrestments and Loosings Thereof, 1767. (Ayrshire Archives, Ayr Burgh Records, B6/15/8)..13

Illus. 6: Demand for payment of duty, including Servant Tax, 1789; issued to Sir Thomas Miller of Barskimming. (Aberdeen University Archives, Special Collections, MS 2769/I/28)..17

Illus. 7: The Feeing Fair at Cumnock (undated). (Courtesy of the Baird Institute, Cumnock) 33

Illus. 8: Notes made by a mistress of Rozelle with a vacancy in her domestic staff (undated). (Ayrshire Archives, Hamilton of Rozelle and Carcluie Papers, SAC/DC/17/27/4/1) 37

Illus. 9: A reference supplied by a Registry. (Ayrshire Archives, Hamilton of Rozelle and Carcluie Papers, SAC/DC/17/27/6/4) 38

Illus. 10: Letter from the General Furnishing Establishment, Ayr. (Ayrshire Archives, Hamilton of Rozelle and Carcluie Papers, SAC/DC/17/27/3/9).....39

Illus. 11: Extract from Aiton's *General View of Agriculture in the County of Ayr*, 1811. 47

Illus. 12: Ayr Advertiser, 6th March 1879. 50

Illus. 13: Account to Robert Burns from Robert Anderson, Shoemaker, Dumfries, 1788. (Courtesy of Peter Westwood) 63

Illus. 14: The staff of Kirkmichael House (undated). (Ayrshire Archives, Kennedy of Kirkmichael papers, ATD 64/11)..65

Illus. 15: A domestic servant on a home visit to her family living in a cottage in the Muirkirk area. (Baird Institute, Cumnock)..66

Illus. 16: Advertisement promoting the sale of clothes for servants which appeared in the *Ayr Post Office General and Trades Directory for Ayr, Newton and Wallacetown* (1912–1913). (Carnegie Library, Ayr)..69

Illus. 17: Extract from the Army & Navy Stores Catalogue, March, 1908. (University of Glasgow Archives, HF6/9/2)..70

Acknowledgements

I wish to express my thanks to the supervisor of the dissertation on which this monograph is based, Professor E.J. Cowan, for the great patience he has shown and the many helpful tips he has provided.

My gratitude is also due to the staff of the following institutions who have so willingly helped me to locate books and documents held in their collections:

University of Glasgow Archives
University of Glasgow Main Library
National Archives of Scotland, Edinburgh
Carnegie Library, Ayr, Local History and Reference Departments
Ayrshire Archives , Ayr
The Mitchell Library, Glasgow
Baird Institute, Cumnock
Dick Institute, Kilmarnock
McKechnie Institute, Girvan
University of Paisley, Craigie Campus, Ayr
Aberdeen University, Special Collections Department
The Savings Bank Museum, Ruthwell, Dumfries

I am grateful too, to the staff of the three Universities, Glasgow, Strathclyde and Stirling who provided training in Research Methods and to Anne Campbell who shared some of her professional knowledge of Scots Law with me.

I wish to thank the many individuals who have lent me books or offered helpful advice when asked. These include Rob Close, Linda Fryer, Margaret Henderson, Alastair Hendry, Jean Hood, Debbie Jackson, Pat McCaig, David McClure and Peter Westwood.

Finally I wish to thank my husband for the many ways in which he has made it possible for me to undertake this study.

Introduction

During the twentieth century, which has been dubbed 'the people's century', there was a growing interest by both professional and amateur historians in how ordinary people lived. Marion Lochhead published *The Scots Household in the Eighteenth Century*[1] which drew on source material from various parts of the country and dealt with people of different status levels, including a nine page chapter on 'Kitchen and Servants'. This was followed by Marjorie Plant's *The Domestic Life of Scotland in the Eighteenth Century*[2], a well researched book, but again based on evidence from localities as far apart as Shetland and Dumfries or St Kilda and Montrose, and dealing with people from all ranks, although servants were studied in greater depth than in Marion Lochhead's book.

Pamela Horn's *The rise and fall of the Victorian servant*[3] published in 1990 was catalogued by the British Library as, 'England, Domestic servants, Conditions of service, History'. This excellent book is full of interesting information, but it deals largely with the English experience, although its bibliography includes the Countess of Aberdeen's advice to servants and their mistresses, also references to a Dundee and a Glasgow newspaper.

In *Farm Servants and Labour in Lowland Scotland 1770–1914*[4] Professor Tom Devine paid tribute to the hard work of the 'in–and–out girls' in his chapter on 'Women Workers 1850–1914'[5]. Despite these various publications there does seem to be a need for a study of servants in a particular locality, covering both domestic and agricultural servants, because in a rural area these may be one and the same, or at least connected to one another by close kinship. For the purpose of this study, south Ayrshire has been taken to comprise the traditional divisions of Kyle and Carrick, as depicted in the maps on pages 9 to 11. This is wider than the both the previous administrative district of 'Kyle and Carrick' and the present administrative district of 'South Ayrshire'.

First, this study is an examination of the relationship between 'society' and the 'lower orders'. How did Church and State seek to control these relationships, and for whose benefit? Did these controls alter over the period? What evidence is there of the actual relationship which existed between particular masters and servants?

Secondly, it is an inquiry into the various methods used by servants to obtain employment and by employers to obtain servants. Following on from this, it is a study of the various conditions of employment and the life styles which servants could expect to follow.

Next, the study attempts to seek evidence of changes in the servant population and to try to explain where possible the reason for these changes. Finally, it deals with some of the factors, which could have had an influence to a greater or lesser degree on the quality of life that a servant could expect.

By piecing together fragmentary references to their lives, it is hoped the patchwork pieces will provide a quilt of knowledge greater than the sum of its parts. Of necessity, it will be incomplete, partly because it has been impossible to trawl through all the sources in the time available, but also because an unquantifiable amount of material is no longer extant, or more likely, was never recorded in the first place. As with any patchwork, there will be pieces which are more colourful than the rest and which help to add interest and give life to the past. They help to illustrate that the servant class was not a homogeneous mass, but a broad section of the total population which contained within it a great number of individual variants, as indeed did 'society' itself.

Pounds, shillings and pence: throughout the period covered by this work, one pound sterling was divided into twenty shillings, and one shilling into twelve pence. They are conventionally represented by £, s and d. Thus £1 13s 6d is one pound thirteen shillings and six pence; 2s 9d is two shillings and nine pence, sometimes shown as 2/9.

[1] Lochhead, Marion, *The Scots Household in the Eighteenth Century* [Edinburgh, 1948]
[2] Plant, Marjorie, *The Domestic Life of Scotland in the 18th Century* [Edinburgh, 1952]
[3] Horn, Pamela, *The Rise and Fall of the Victorian Servant* [Stroud, 1990]
[4] Devine, T.M., *Farm Servants and Labour in Lowland Scotland 1770–1914* [Edinburgh, 1984]
[5] *ibid*, p. 109.

Illus. 1: Map of the County of Ayr, Sayer & Bennett, November 1777.

Illus. 2: Cunninghame.

Illus. 3: Kyle.

Illus. 4: Carrick.

Note: The sectional maps of Cunninghame, Kyle and Carrick have been enlarged to fit the page width, and are not to the same scale.

Chapter 1: The Master–Servant Relationship

The master–servant relationship as defined in law

According to Erskine's *Principles of the Law of Scotland,*

> A servant is one who agrees to give his services to another for a
> determinate time and at an ascertained hire. He differs – in so far as a
> distinction can be drawn – from an agent, in being paid wages, not
> commission, and from a contractor employed to do a piece of work, in being
> bound not only to do his work, but also to follow his employer's orders in
> the doing of it.[1]

Whereas Erskine distinguished a servant from an agent or a contractor,
Viscount Stair, some two centuries earlier, traced the process from slavery to
bondage to the status of servant.

> Servants with us, which now retain that name, are judged free
> persons, and have at most but hired their labour to their masters for a time,
> which is a kind of contract betwixt them.[2]

Although these definitions would exclude from the servant class,
professional people such as lawyers and physicians, and business people including
tenant farmers, almost the entire working population could be included. For the
purpose of this study, the term *servant* has been limited to domestic and
agricultural servants, who in a largely rural society were often one and the same,
particularly in the case of female servants. This accords with G. J. Bell's clear
statement in 1839 regarding the hiring of domestic servants. 'This is a contract for
the hire of services to be performed in the domestic economy of a house, garden, or
farm or in personal attendance.'[3]

Prior to the 1707 Act of Union, the parliaments of Scotland had over the
centuries, established laws relating to master and servant, and this legislation
remained in force after the Union. Subsequent legislation was enacted by the
United Kingdom parliament and was largely designed to amend English law. In
the absence of parliamentary interest in Scots law for almost two hundred years
after the Union, the Scottish courts interpreted the existing law. The condition of
desuetude applied if it could 'be shown that the offence is not only practised
without being checked, but is no longer considered or dealt with in this country as
an offence against the law.'[4]

Seventeenth century legislation gave the Justices of the Peace the power, at
their quarter sessions in August and February, 'to fix the ordinary wages of
workmen, labourers and servants, to imprison such as refuse to serve for the
appointed hire, and to compel payment by the masters.'[5] There is evidence to

show that servants could be imprisoned for failing to serve for the appointed hire as in the following example,

> Air June 1ˢᵗ 1767
>
> Then the Person of David Kaithness was incarserate within the Tolbooth of Ayr by virtue of a Warrand from William Logan Sheriff Subt of Ayr dated the twenty ninth day of may seventeen hundred and sixty seven years. Proceeding upon the petition of John Hamilton of Sundrum Esqr addressed to the said William Logan agt the said David Kaithness in which Tolbooth he shall remain until he find Caution that he shall return to the said John Hamilton's service which warrand is put up amongst the Town's papers.
>
> Ayr 5ᵗʰ June 1767
>
> Then the Person of David Kaithness late Cook with John Hamilton of Sundrum who was incarserate within the Tolbooth of Ayr the first June Current was liberate furth of the said tolbooth in consequence of a letter from John Hamilton of Sundrum at whose instance he was incarserate which letter is put amongst the towns papers.[6]

Farm servants could be compelled to serve for a year rather than from Martinmas (11th November) to Whitsunday (15th May). The remaining six months of the year was the season when there was a high demand for labour on the land with crops to sow, raise and harvest. It was also the season when work was more readily available for such diverse tasks as, 'casting and winning peats, turfs, 'fail divots' (turf cut for building or roofing), building dykes, shearing corn.'[7] Servants would often seek higher wages to serve from Whitsunday to Martinmas, or they would remain unbound and work casually to further their own interests. Farmers would therefore be economically disadvantaged either by having to pay higher wages, or by experiencing a shortage of labour. To counter these difficulties, the legislation required that, 'employers may compel loose and masterless men and women whom they find on their bounds to work.'[8]

Idle beggars and vagabonds and disobedient servants could be corrected and put to work by the Master of the Correction House. The law required, 'Masters of correction–houses to receive disobedient servants, force them to work, and correct them according to their demerits.'[9] Numerous incarcerations of vagrants in the Tolbooth of Ayr are recorded in the 'Burgh Register of Incarcerations, Liberations and Arrestments and Loosings Thereof' which is extant from 1742. Unfortunately, the eighteenth century town papers so frequently referred to in this register have not survived, so that the details of the various cases remain unknown.

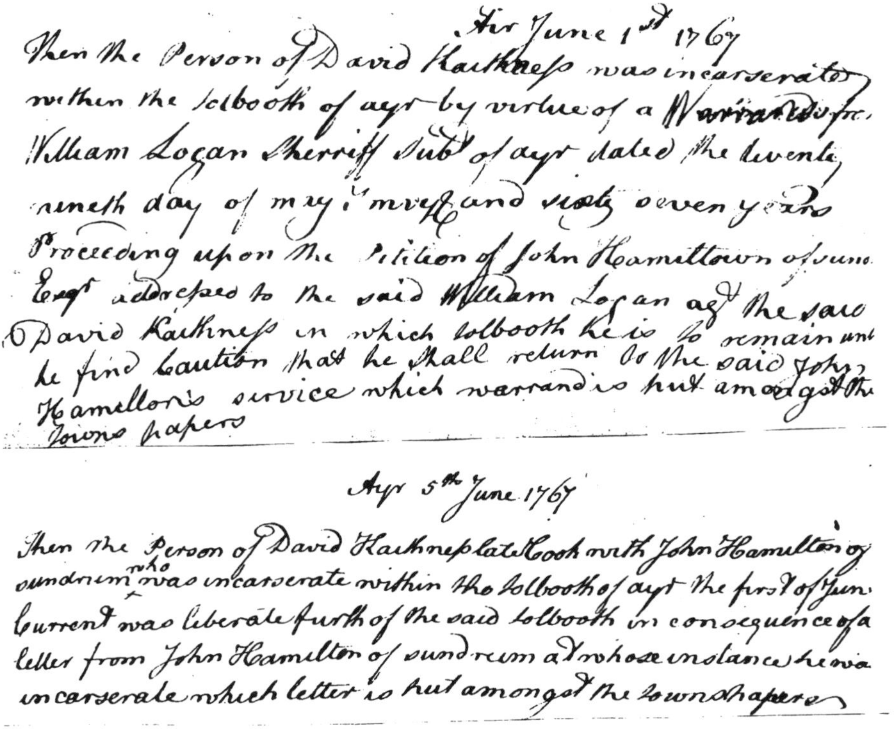

[Handwritten text, reading:]

Ayr June 1st 1767

Then the Person of David Kauthness was incarserate within the Tolbooth of ayr by virtue of a Warrand &c. William Logan Sherriff Sub of ayr dated the twenty nineth day of may mveß and sixty seven years Proceeding upon the Petition of John Hamilltown of sundrum Esqr adcrefsed to the said William Logan agt the said David Kauthness in which tolbooth he is to remain until he find Caution that he shall return to the said John Hamilton's service which warrand is hut amongst the Towns papers

Ayr 5th June 1767

Then the Person of David Kauthness late Cook with John Hamilton of sundrum who was incarserate within the Tolbooth of ayr the first of Jun current was liberate furth of the said Tolbooth in consequence of a letter from John Hamilton of sundrum at whose instance he was incarserate which letter is hut amongst the Towns papers

Illus. 5:   Extracts from Ayr Burgh Register of Incarcerations, Liberations and Arrestments and Loosings Thereof, 1767. (Ayrshire Archives, Ayr Burgh Records, B6/15/8)

Another measure which prohibited 'salmon fishing or any other labour on the Lord's Day not only extends to servants who actually work, but also to masters whose hired servants they are, if the masters know or connive at their working.'[10] In January 1750, the kirk session of Dailly parish was much concerned with the case of James MacCrae, servant to John McAdam of Craigangillan who,

> a minute or two before the ringing of the third bell advanced to the Kirk–post with a drove of black cattle and being driven back by the inhabitants of the parish, stopt the ringing of the bell and went forward being met by the Minr. and others it was observed that William Baird, servant to Gilbert Muir merchant in Dailly went along from the kirk helping forward the drove.[11]

The matter was referred to the Presbytery of Ayr, but Baird ignored the three summons he received to compear before that body. There is no record of any action before a civil court since the records of the local Justices of the Peace are no longer extant.

The employment of Roman Catholics as servants was not generally permitted. The 1696 Act stated:

> If a protestant in a popish family becomes a papist, the servant shall
> be punished as an apostate; the papist master to dismiss the servant, who
> shall not be received again by him nor by any other popish master under
> penalties; protestant servants to attend divine service and catechising.[12]

Further legislation stipulated 'no papist to be entertained as a domestic servant by a protestant.'[13] The regulation of servants' clothing was also the subject of legislation.[14] This will be explained in a later chapter.

Although the records of the Ayrshire Justices of the Peace are no longer extant, on occasion the surviving kirk session minutes refer to regulations imposed by the justices, as for example the vagrancy regulations quoted in the Dailly Kirk Session Minutes of 29th May 1752.[15] In 1751, justices drew up 'Regulations for Farm Servants in Dumfries–shire' and it is probable that similar regulations existed in neighbouring Ayrshire.[16] Wages in both cash and kind were to be controlled, with fines imposed on both master and servant for exceeding the set level. Furthermore, informers were to be rewarded.

Servants were obliged to serve the full year for which they had been contracted, 'unless when sufficient cause can be shown before some of the Justices.' No such escape clause was provided for the servant but, where master and servant agreed, the contract could be terminated at the end of six months. Domestic servants, both male and female, could not offer themselves for hire before the first day of both March and September to start employment on Whitsunday and Martinmas respectively. The penalty for contravention was a fine of half a year's fee for both master and servant, the agreement to be declared null and void and such further proceedings taken, 'as the Justices shall think fit.' Here again, there was an escape clause, 'excepting always that masters may hire their own servants at any time.' Presumably this referred to such personal servants as valets and lady's maids. Great attention was given to the shortage of good servants and frequent inclination for them to indulge in idleness. To combat this, the Justices ordained that domestic servants employed by farmers required a licence from two Justices of the Peace in order to take up other employment. Non–compliance carried a fine of twenty shillings sterling and the obligation to serve as a domestic servant for one year 'to any person who shall apply to the Justice of the Peace for that purpose.' Furthermore, unless a domestic servant was gainfully employed, or had a licence from the Justices, or was unfit, he or she could be compelled to serve any employer requiring a servant. Failure to comply meant prosecution. Servants wishing to leave their situation had to give three months notice before two witnesses, or continue in the service for a further year. Similarly, masters were required to give three months notice before two witnesses when they wished to dispense with the services of a servant. To encourage servants, the justices enacted measures to require masters to pay fees punctually. On the other hand all persons with the capacity or ability to serve were to find employment, or be classed as vagabonds and incarcerated until such times as they became employed.[17]

Prior to 1799, colliers and salters could be bought and sold together with the mine in which they worked, which was a form of slavery. There were salt pans in both Ayr and Prestwick and coal pits in a number of south Ayrshire locations. In addition there were a few cases of negro slaves, brought to Ayrshire estates, whose status then became that of servant instead of slave. For example, there is the well documented case of Scipio Kennedy from Guinea, taken to the West Indies as a slave, given his freedom at Culzean in 1725, and who remained there in service until his death in June 1774.[18] Or that of a 'Black Boy' employed as a servant by Mungo Smith Esq of Drongan from 1777–1779.[19] There may also have been black servants at Sundrum, for according to Shaw, who gave no indication as to the source of this material,

> In the village of Joppa on the main road from Ayr to Cumnock there were at one time a number of negroes brought from the plantations in West Indies, belonging to John Hamilton of Sundrum. They intermarried with the local inhabitants, and traces of negro in the hair and countenance could be observed for some generations.[20]

In order to raise money for the wars fought during the reign of George III, taxes were levied on masters and mistresses employing servants. The tax applied to the employment of male servants from 1777–1792, and to female servants from 1785–1792. The tax levied varied from year to year, with bachelor masters paying additional tax. There were exemptions for servants employed in husbandry, manufacture, and any trade or calling by which the employer gained a livelihood. Also, for every two children under the age of fourteen living in the household, one female servant could be employed without a tax liability. 'Any officer under the Rank of Field Officer, or not receiving the Pay of a Field Officer, could retain one servant without paying duty.'[21] Duty was payable on servants retained or employed as Maitre d'Hotel, House–steward, Master of the Horse, Groom of the Chamber, Valet de Chambre, Butler, Under–butler, Clerk of the Kitchen, Confectioner, Cook, House–porter, Footman, Running Footman, Coachman, Groom, Postilion, Stable–boy, Helpers in Stables, Gardener not being a Day–

Labourer, Park–keeper, Gamekeeper, Huntsman or Whipper–in, Waiters in Taverns, Coffee–houses, Inns, Alehouses.

It was also payable on female servants, although their job description was not stated. Employers were required to make an annual return to the Surveyor of Taxes, who in the case of Ayrshire was Mr Aitken of Ayr. In February 1786, when at Mossgiel, Robert Burns replied to his tax mandate with the poem, *The Inventory*.

> For men, I've three mischievous boys,
> Run de'ils for rantin' an for noise;
> A gaudsman ane, a thrasher t'other,
> Wee Davock hauds the nowte in father.

According to the extant tax returns, he did not pay tax on his servants either in Ayrshire or Dumfriesshire.

The estate of Barskimming, in the parish of Stair, was the property of Sir Thomas Miller, Bart who in his capacity of President of the Court of Session and Lord Justice Clerk, spent much of his time in Edinburgh where he paid the tax for his servants.[22] Two years later, the tax records show that his son William, having inherited the property on his father's death, paid tax in Ayrshire for his gamekeeper, James McKerrow at Barskimming.[23] Although the tax was paid by the employer, it did have a consequence for the servants themselves. An entry from the Culzean accounts reads,

> Mart 28 85. Betty Trail and Jack do all the Porter's work. These wages together come only to ½ a porter's wage besides the Difference between the tax of a man servant and a maid and the maid spins and does other work.[24]

This surely could not have been the only case of an employer who was influenced by this tax.

The Truck Acts of the nineteenth century, which applied to those engaged in manual labour and therefore members of the servant class in the legal sense, did not apply to domestic servants. Theoretically, a servant could bring an action for damages against an employer's material breach of contract or an unjustifiable dismissal. However, in the case of a domestic servant being ill–treated, the servant had to leave the employment, for by staying on it would be held that he or she had abandoned any claim for damage.[25]

There cannot have been many servants with the financial resources to enable them to seek legal redress even when their case was deserving. Furthermore, there were often considerable difficulties for the domestic servant if required to leave the post at short notice. Where was another post to be found which would offer not only wages, but board and lodging when, in all probability, the servant would not have been able to give a reference by an alleged unscrupulous employer? This would be a particular consideration where the servant had no family or friends to provide temporary shelter.

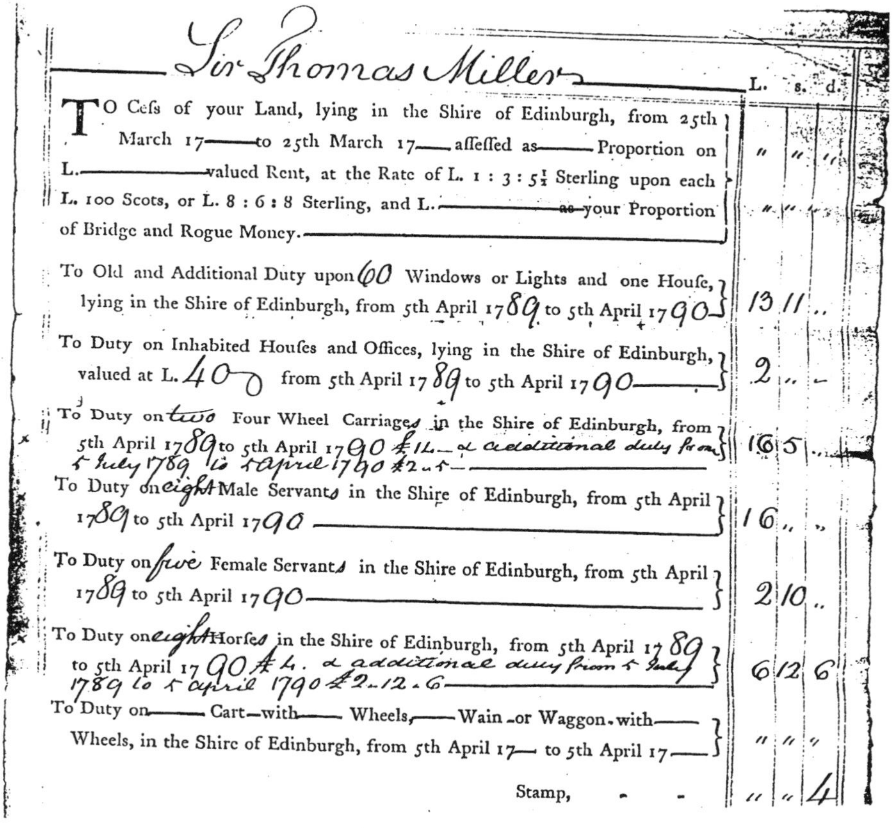

Sir Thomas Miller

	L.	s.	d.
TO Cess of your Land, lying in the Shire of Edinburgh, from 25th March 17—to 25th March 17— assessed as— Proportion on L.—valued Rent, at the Rate of L. 1 : 3 : 5½ Sterling upon each L. 100 Scots, or L. 8 : 6 : 8 Sterling, and L.— as your Proportion of Bridge and Rogue Money.—	"	"	"
To Old and Additional Duty upon 60 Windows or Lights and one House, lying in the Shire of Edinburgh, from 5th April 1789 to 5th April 1790	13	11	..
To Duty on Inhabited Houses and Offices, lying in the Shire of Edinburgh, valued at L. 40 from 5th April 1789 to 5th April 1790—	2	..	–
To Duty on two Four Wheel Carriages in the Shire of Edinburgh, from 5th April 1789 to 5th April 1790 £14 – & additional duty from 5 July 1789 to 5 April 1790 £2.5 –	16	5	..
To Duty on eight Male Servants in the Shire of Edinburgh, from 5th April 1789 to 5th April 1790 —	16	..	..
To Duty on five Female Servants in the Shire of Edinburgh, from 5th April 1789 to 5th April 1790—	2	10	..
To Duty on eight Horses in the Shire of Edinburgh, from 5th April 1789 to 5th April 1790 £4. & additional duty from 5 July 1789 to 5 April 1790 £2.12.6	6	12	6
To Duty on— Cart—with— Wheels,—Wain—or Waggon—with— Wheels, in the Shire of Edinburgh, from 5th April 17— to 5th April 17—	"	"	"
Stamp, - -	"	"	4

Illus. 6: Demand for payment of duty, including Servant Tax, 1789; issued to Sir Thomas Miller of Barskimming. (Aberdeen University Archives, Special Collections, MS 2769/I/28.

The Reform Act of 1832 was a step on the road to securing a democratic form of government for the country, but the qualifications required by the act excluded the entire servant class from the franchise. Even the 1868 Act would have done little for the bulk of servants. It was not until the Third Reform Act of 1884 that the male franchise was widened. But women had to wait until after the First World War had ended before they were to secure the vote, as had male 'servants living in, sons living at home, soldiers in barracks, those in receipt of poor relief, and those who had not paid their rates.'[26] The consequence of this piecemeal reform of the voting system meant that the law governing the relationship between masters and servants was proposed and enacted by representatives of the dominant class in society and, however benevolent some of these lawmakers may have been, the majority of them must have tended to view the regulation of behaviour from their own perspective, as had been the case traditionally.

The master–servant relationship as recommended by the Church

In an age when a huge swathe of the population have no Church connection, or at best pay lip–service at Christmas time, or use the Church to give social cachet to their rites of passage, it is perhaps difficult to appreciate the extent to which the Church regulated people's lives in the period covered by this study.

Education was largely provided by the Church until 1872 when the state took over the responsibility to provide primary education for all children.[27]

Providing for the needs of the poor and the infirm was a constant responsibility of the Church. When the ability of the parishes to raise money was outstripped by the needs of the parishioners in the nineteenth century, Poor Law legislation instituted the transfer of the responsibility from the Church to the civic authorities.

Through its courts, the Church exercised control over the populace and determined the prevailing ethos, which in general was in accord with the wishes of the heritors, who exercised their powers of patronage to appoint ministers of the established church, rented land to the tenant farmers, and in some cases either they or their factors sat as members of the courts. The general assemblies of both the established and free churches passed acts which were implemented by the kirk sessions with the guidance of the presbytery in complex or disputed cases. The minutes of the various kirk sessions provide a catalogue of the misdemeanours of those who compeared before them, the majority of whom were of the 'lower orders', though sometimes tenant farmers or their offspring were involved.

Fornication, especially when it resulted in an illegitimate birth, was generally the most frequent type of case with which a kirk session had to deal. Membership of a kirk session doubtless afforded opportunities for obsessive misogynists to exploit their prejudices, or for others to revel in vicarious sex when dealing with such cases, but usually financial considerations were behind the inquiries. Until the 1840s, the sessions were responsible for the support of the poor from often inadequate funds. It was, therefore, necessary to deter unmarried persons from producing illegitimate children or, when strictures failed in this respect, to pursue all avenues to find the responsible father in order to urge him to contribute to the maintenance of the child. Furthermore, by publicly shaming the guilty parties, it was hoped to deter them and others from further scandals. A need to arrest the spread of disease such as syphilis might also have contributed to the often rigid efforts to control sexual morals. Doubtless too, many of the fathers and brethren may have honestly held beliefs that their inquisitorial hearing of cases involving sexual irregularities was in accord with Christian teaching.

Other matters subject to the attention of the kirk sessions included violation of the Sabbath, the preliminary hearing of adultery cases, irregular marriage, minor cases of public disorder and, in the interest of community harmony, helping to resolve local disputes.

The ministers and elders of the kirk made regular checks to ascertain that the catechism was taught and adhered to. Robert Burns spent his Sunday evenings making sure that his servants were well versed in their knowledge of the Shorter Catechism[28] as no doubt did the majority of local farmers. Nevertheless, there was a back–sliding to the extent that in 1834 the General Assembly of the Church of Scotland issued a pastoral admonition to be publicly read by all its ministers. It was concerned with the failure to keep the Sabbath in the proper manner. One of the reasons given for this fall in standards was ascribed to 'the inattention of the masters to the spiritual welfare of their servants.' Parents and masters were exhorted to ensure that their children and then all the other members of the household should follow biblical teachings in preference to 'their own pleasure.' Instruction was to be given and example set in order to demonstrate how reasonable, beneficial and pleasing 'the duties of devotion were . . . having promise of life that now is, and which is to come.' A reciprocal exhortation followed, addressed to 'the humble in station.'[29]

An example of the Sabbath being broken has been quoted previously. As might be expected, William Baird, the Dailly merchant's servant, was cited to appear before the local kirk session, and James MacCrae, his accomplice, and the servant of John McAdam, a proprietor of land in the parish of Straiton, was the subject of a letter written by the minister of Dailly parish to the minister of Straiton parish. It seems to have been quite customary for sessions to correspond with each other, through their ministers or session clerks, in order to ensure that delinquents were not easily able to avoid censure for their misconduct.[30]

Another entry from the same parish records, dated 24th January 1813, states that James Ferguson and William Kennedy confessed that 'they were guilty of intemperance, quarrelling, and fighting on a Sabbath morning.' On 27th April 1840, also in Dailly,

> The Moderator stated that he had called this meeting because it was generally known that an arrangement was made by some inhabitants of the village on the evening of the preceding Sabbath to fight a battle which actually came off on Monday and he considered it right that some inquiry should be made into the particulars of so disgraceful a proceeding. The session highly approved of this being done and after some conversation

directed their officer to summon Thomas Dodds before them on May 5th current at one o'clock.

No further mention was made of this inquiry, but the entry indicates the importance of the Church in dealing with matters like public order in a rural community at that time.

Occasionally accusations of quite mundane affairs could lead to further revelations. On June 16th 1765, Samuel Brown and Margaret Niven appeared before Kirkoswald Kirk Session charged with the sin of fornication before marriage. They were exhorted and examined as usual in these cases but 'The Session were informed that the above Samuel Brown gave public offence by violating the Sabbath Day in the month of October last.'[31] They decided that before granting him absolution, the moderator should further interrogate him. This led to revelations about a smuggling incident in the Turnberry quarter of the parish, which involved a great many people, both masters and servants. All the participants were named, and interrogated, their testimony providing a graphic account of the event. The session's sole concern was in establishing '[w]hat persons were guilty of any profanation upon said Day.' It mattered not to them whether the participants were assisting Archibald Ritchie, Commander of the King's 'whirrey' (wherry) to guard the 'Counterband goods', or were colluding with the two Manx men. For whatever reason, the session had its own priorities.

In October 1858 the Free Church issued a Pastoral Address targeting the consciences of employers. They were reminded that domestic servants were to be regarded as part of their family, and as such, masters and mistresses had a responsibility for both their spiritual and temporal welfare. They were to be 'instructed, watched over, guarded from temptation, directed, encouraged in duty, led to feel that they have an interest in the religion, and the religious duties of the family.'[32] The address carried on to include consideration for cottagers, farm workers, farm servants, workers in mines, shops of the different trades, shop–assistants and clerks. To balance this, domestics and other employees were reminded of what duties were required of them, namely, 'faithfulness, conscientious service — not eye–service merely — truth, civility, a studying the interest of their master or mistress, or employer.' They were expected to be thankful when they found themselves employed in a desirable situation and when this was not the case, they were to endure the circumstances patiently until their contract expired, remembering that they were giving service to God not man.

In 1862, a further pastoral address was issued to 'Masters and Servants in the Families under their Care.'[33] It began by acknowledging the 'commercial character' of the relationship, 'of parties entering into a legal contract–work and wages for work.' It pointed out that this distinguished the relationship from that pertaining to 'slavery and serfdom of other times and lands.' It then went on to enumerate the duties towards their servants of masters, who were advised 'to take a deep interest in the comfort, health and well being of their servants.' They were to pray for them, and a master was further advised to 'take a deep interest in the religious instruction of his servants.' They were to treat servants with kindness and courtesy and 'to notice, encourage and command service thoroughly and conscientiously done.' Finally, masters were reminded that 'it is the duty of the master, while maintaining a due order and discipline in his household, *to impose no needless restraints on the freedom of his servants.*'

Provision was to be made for servants to attend church at a time suitable to the employing family, but servants were not 'to spend their Sabbath evenings in visiting friends, or in other ways of which the master has and takes no knowledge.' This practice was considered to be 'full of danger and mischief to servants themselves.' Instead it was recommended that the 'time–honoured practice of family catechising were resumed among us.' The points raised in the 1862 address were essentially a restructuring of the 1858 address.

In the second part of the address, servants' duties were listed and expanded with a liberal scattering of biblical references furnished in order to provide a greater degree of authority. They were told that 'it is their duty to do the work of their particular place thoroughly, conscientiously and with all good fidelity.' Servants were reminded 'of the duty of a respectful, quiet and modest demeanour in their whole intercourse of communication with their masters and counselled 'to take an interest in the well–being and comfort, and good name, of the families where they serve,' and pray for them. The fifth duty was specifically addressed to female servants. They were to 'guard against all levity of spirit and demeanour, all undue freedoms of the other sex, everything which is not in full keeping with the purity and gravity of Christian discipleship.' Also, they were cautioned against the wearing of 'a style of dress unsuitable to your station, too gay and showy.' Referring to the interest that masters were to take in the religious instruction of their servants, it was to be a corresponding duty of servants 'gratefully and cordially to accept that interest, and all suitable manifestations of it.' Finally, servants had the duty 'of cultivating by every possible means an unbroken peace among themselves.' In support of all these counsels, a range of biblical texts were cited, namely 'Ephesians vi, 5–8; Colossians iii, 22–24; Titus ii, 9–14; 2 Peter ii, 18–25 and Genesis xxiv.' The 67 verses of the Genesis chapter telling about the servant of Abraham who was entrusted with the task of selecting a wife for Abraham's son were thought to contain examples of how a master could trust a servant, and how such a trusted servant should act. It would seem that the Free Church was promoting a paternalistic relationship between masters and servants.

An examination of the *Acts of the General Assembly* of the Church of Scotland from 1705–1870 fails to reveal similar guidance concerning the inter–personal relationships between masters and servants. Possibly the assumption was made that such relationships would follow traditional custom and habit. The

Established Church issued a 'Pastoral Letter to the People of Scotland on Family Worship' on May 1836, which was prefixed to the 'Family Prayers' prepared by the Committee on Aids to Devotion in 1865 and reprinted in a cheap edition in 1869.[34]

During the 1860s, the Established Church became greatly preoccupied with the increase of immorality in the rural districts. In the Assembly's Pastoral Address of 1861, advice was given to landlords, farmers and others employing the agricultural population seriously to consider what prudent measures they could adopt in the provision of dwellings and accommodation for their servants.[35] They were also urged to exercise 'a kindly superintendence over the young of both sexes, as well during the hours of labour, as in the time of rest and recreation.' This was to discourage 'opportunities for loose conversation and other temptations to sin.' The young, especially the females, were to learn, and have respect for, 'delicacy and virtue.'

Three decades later, there must still have been cause for concern, for in May 1897, the General Assembly of the Free Church, commended its Special Report on 'The Religious and Moral Conditions of Farm Servants' to its presbyteries. They were instructed 'to look into the condition of the rural population within their bounds, and to take such action to remedy existing evils.'[36]

The vast majority of the cases dealt with by the kirk sessions were of a sexual nature, hence the concerns of the General Assemblies. Examples of these cases in Ayrshire will be provided in a later chapter.

The master–servant relationship in practice

Whereas the Master–Servant relationship required by law and fostered by the Church in Scotland is fairly well documented, trying to find evidence of how these relationships worked out in practice is, as one would expect, like looking for the proverbial needle in a hay–stack, particularly from the servant's point of view.

An indication of what must have been a prevailing attitude among 'society' of the time, is provided in John Galt's novel *The Member* when the character Archibald Jobbry MP, prior to the 1832 Reform Bill, says to himself,

> I have heard most intelligent men in India say, that the order of castes, though a different kind, prevailed as strikingly in England as among the Hindoos, . . . even Nature seems herself to minister to this; for just look at the stout, short, civil, spirited little men that she breed for grooms and servants, and compare them with the tall, lank, genteel aristocracy of their masters.[37]

Whether the physical characteristics of the two classes of people compared here were in fact correct, the perception that there were innate differences between those born to follow and those born to lead ran deep in society.

John MacDonald's *Memoirs of a Eighteenth Century Footman* provides some clues, although it reads more like an eighteenth century novel than a memoir of his life and travels.[38]

In his account, he first arrived at Bargany from Edinburgh in 1750 at the age of nine dressed in his new postilion's livery, having just been hired by the Bargany coachman for the wage of two pounds a year, all his clothes and a third part of the vails (tips).

On arrival, he was taken into the parlour to meet Lady Anne Hamilton to see if she liked him. She admired his livery and his littleness, which must have been important considerations for the job. After two days, during which he tended a sick horse that he had ridden from Edinburgh, he returned there with the three horses which had been hired to help pull the new heavy carriage to Bargany. It seems a formidable task to ask a nine–year–old to take three horses such a long way on his own and to handle the money for both the hire of the horses and for the expenses of the horses at the same inns on both the outward and return journeys.

A month later he returned to Bargany where he stayed for six years before being hired by the Earl of Craufurd to drive the post chaises and four horses and to have charge of the saddle–horses for which his wages were five pounds. He had sought this new position because for years he had been ill–treated by the Bargany coachman. When, too late, Lady Anne learned of this, she is reputed to have said to her maid, 'if I had known, I would have brought John MacDonald up to be my footman, and not to be used as he has been by John Bell.'

Later, in his new position, he reported that Lady Craufurd remarked, 'I don't wonder that it is reported Jack MacDonald's father was a captain in the Prince's army, for he certainly is some gentleman's son or some nobleman's bastard.' He also claimed that, 'if any person spoke against me to my Lord or herself, she told me who the person was, because I saved her daughter, Lady Jane, from the flames.' This was a reference to the fire which burned down Kilbirnie Castle in May 1757. Other accounts of this fire attribute the rescue of the young child to the earl himself, but it is possible that a servant did play a prominent part despite the credit having been given to the nobleman.

In November 1759, he left his service because, he said, 'My Lord began to dislike me, and for which I was very sorry – and, my readers, I cannot tell you for what.' It is possible that the earl himself was a difficult person to relate to, for at a later stage, the earl and the countess separated and there is ample evidence in the Rozelle papers to show that the countess's father took her part in the matrimonial dispute. On the other hand, a chamber maid at Bargany later told a visiting lady guest, 'As you know, madam, the Earl and Countess have been parted almost a twelvemonth, and I dare say, you have heard for what.' This remark was alluding to the reputation which John MacDonald was acquiring as a philanderer.

In 1760, he had been again hired by John Hamilton of Bargany, this time as his body servant. However, Lady Anne found it necessary to dispense with the services of the housekeeper and a chambermaid, and to ask her own god–daughter and an innocent lady guest to leave the house because she thought there was something between them and John MacDonald. When his services were dispensed with, he found it difficult to obtain another place because of his reputation with the ladies, and had eventually to serve as valet to a bachelor household in London, which John Hamilton, having parted with his wife, visited and blamed him for being the first to take up with Lady Anne. In this case, MacDonald claimed to be innocent which was probably so, for he was not shy about claiming his sexual conquests.

As one can see from this abbreviated section of the memoir, the relationship between the gentry and their personal servants could encompass emotions like jealousy and sexual desire. Undoubtedly, John MacDonald was a unique character in many ways, but one can see that there was scope for difficulties to arise, particularly when a servant was both personable and intelligent.

Women servants were particularly vulnerable to the sexual appetites of their masters or their masters' sons. Kirkmichael Kirk Session and Ayr Presbytery[39] were concerned with the case of Captain Bell of Arnsow, a married man, who in 1780 was cited as being responsible for the pregnancy of his former servant Janet McMurtrie. In a letter dated 17th January 1781, he declined to accept the jurisdiction of the session on the grounds that on accepting his army commission he had been required to become a member of the established Church of England. In May 1781, Elizabeth Neil, another Arnsow servant, was reputed to be with child, and in July 1781, she too cited Captain Bell as being responsible for her condition.[40] The case dragged on through the summer, Captain Bell still not acknowledging the session's jurisdiction, and also denying responsibility for fathering Elizabeth Neil's child. She, on the other hand, claimed that he had proposed she should go to Edinburgh to see Dr Primrose who would 'take care of her,' but she had been prevented from this course of action by her friends. She further claimed that when the child was born, he sent his man–servant to see what the child was like. She owned to have received a guinea from Captain Bell who had asked that the child be named James and had agreed to pay the nurse's fee when the child was a 'quarter old'.

She declared that Mrs Bell had been fully aware of her husband's guilt, wished it to be concealed, and had advised her to agree to the proposed Edinburgh scheme. In October 1781, Elizabeth Neil declared her intention of taking her case to a civil court, and the session postponed further action. Three years later,[41] she again appeared before the session and related that she had left the service of Captain Frock in Irvine the previous Martinmas, without telling him that he was responsible for her pregnancy. She went to serve in Barr, but left in March and gave birth to her child in the Gorbals of Glasgow. The next day she set out for Ayrshire, attempted to abandon her child in Riccartoun, but was prevented by the minister there. The child was now being nursed by Margaret McCollouch. The session referred the case to the Irvine Kirk Session. In February 1797, she gave birth to yet another child, this time naming a married man in Straiton,[42] Andrew McWhirter, which he denied and the session decided to delay the matter for some time. It may be that Elizabeth Neil was promiscuous, but it seems more likely that she was exploited by her masters.

Sixty years later, in May 1857, Dankeith House in Symington was rented by the lady who was to become the wife of Dr Story. In *Early Reminiscences,* Janet Story recalled engaging:

> A Jack–of–all–trades as a coachman who was to be a valet to gentlemen when not required, assist in waiting at table and work in the garden when his other avocations permitted any leisure. I may mention that they never did, and I discovered that his ample leisure was chiefly occupied in playing cards with a good–looking parlour–maid whom he afterwards married.[43]

This was probably a fairly typical view that an employer might hold. However, she also provided a glowing picture of another of her servants:

> We have got a girl as a sort of 'orra girl', to fetch the milk and letters and generally assist the cook and other servants. She comes from this neighbourhood; her father is a gamekeeper and she is perfectly lovely; just seventeen, tall with the figure of a nymph, quantities of golden hair, a skin like milk and eyes like the pearls of a forget–me–not. I never saw anyone more exquisite and when she is about I cannot take my eyes from her face.[44]

During her stay at Dankeith, she was on one occasion invited to stay a few days at a friend's house. On the Sunday, her hostess advised her to eat a good breakfast, as only a light lunch would be served. This proved to be a bowl of potatoes, which was ordered by the hostess, 'out of consideration for her servants, as the cook was enabled thereby to attend church.'[45]

In her *Later Reminiscences,* she mentioned a servant who had been with her for nearly forty years, at a time when other ladies were complaining about the difficulty of obtaining good servants. This was in 1894.[46] Did this say something about how well or not employers and servants were able to form mutually satisfactory relationships with each other?

The Ayrshire Sound Archive includes an interview with Mrs Hume who was the cook at Bargany. She started working at Bargany as a 15–year–old scullery maid and described those times. She recalled that 'Lord Stair insisted his servants got dinner before him on Sunday, that he could wait because they had been working.'[47]   Mrs Hume went on to comment, 'You know they had consideration in ways.'

> Each person knew what to do. I wouldn't have dared go up to Cook. You waited until you were spoken to. Cook was your mistress. She kept her place and you kept yours. She was nice to you in a way. Every morning the scullery maid took a big ewer of water up to the cook's bedroom – no bathrooms. Sometimes she would say, 'is there a cup of tea going?' But not often. But lots of them did like a cup of tea.

This interview would indicate that in a large establishment it was not only the relationship between master and servant that mattered but the relationships between senior and junior members of the domestic staff as well.

It would appear that the master–servant relationship was not only governed by the prevailing structures of the law and the contemporary ethos engendered by the Church, but above all by the unequal inter–personal relationships which existed in practice, with the balance of power tilted very considerably in favour of the master or mistress.   At best the servant could be the recipient of benevolent paternalism, at worst the victim of sexual abuse.

There are many different definitions and understandings of the status of the servant. This chapter has examined the legal definitions, the view of the Church and such examples of everyday relationships as are available.

[1] Erskine, John, *Principles of the Law of Scotland* [Edinburgh, 1890]
[2] Stair, James, Viscount of, *The Institutions of the Law of Scotland*, 1693, Walker, David M, ed., [Edinburgh & Glasgow, 1981]
[3] Bell, George, Joseph, *Principles of the Laws of Scotland* [Edinburgh, 1839]
[4] Watson, George, *Bell's Dictionary and Digest of the Law of Scotland Adapted to the Present State of the Law and in Great Part Re–Written* [London, 1882]
[5] Acts of the Parliaments of Scotland (hereafter A.P.S.)1617, IV 537; A.P.S. 1661, VII 308.
[6] Ayrshire Archives (hereafter A.A.), Ayr Burgh Register of Incarcerations, Liberations and Arrestments and Loosings Thereof, B6/15/8.
[7] A.P.S. 1621, IV 623.
[8] *ibid.*
[9] A.P.S. 1672, VIII 91a.
[10] A.P.S. 1644, VII 194.
[11] A.A., Dailly Kirk Session Minutes. CH2/392/2.
[12] A.P.S. 1696, X 64.
[13] A.P.S. 1700, X 218b.
[14] A.P.S. 1621, 1V 626.
[15] A.A., Dailly Kirk Session Minutes. CH2/392/2.
[16] M'Diarmid, W.R., "The Regulation of Farm Servants in Dumfries–shire in 1751" in *The Transactions & Journal of the Proceedings of the Dumfries & Galloway Natural History & Antiquarian Society* Vol.2, Session 1864–65, p. 37.
[17] *ibid* p.37–41.

[18] National Archives of Scotland (hereafter N.A.S.), Ailsa Muniments GD 25/9/72/9.

[19] N.A.S., Servant Tax Returns 1777–1778, E326/5/1; 1778–1779, E326/5/3.

[20] Shaw, James Edward, *Ayrshire, 1745–1950, A Social and Industrial History,* [Edinburgh & London, 1953], p. 23.

[21] *Duties on Servants,* 25 Geo. 3 c.43, 1785.

[22] Aberdeen University, Special Collections, *Miller of Glenlee,* MS 2769/1/28/1–3.

[23] N.A.S., Servant Tax Return, 1792–1793, E326/5/19.

[24] N.A.S., Ailsa Muniments, GD25/9/19.

[25] Gloag & Henderson *Introduction to the Law of Scotland* (fifth edition) [Edinburgh, 1952] edition by Gibb & Walker p. 223.

[26] Smout, T.C., *A History of the Scottish People 1830–1950* [London, 1971], p. 246.

[27] Cruickshank, Marjorie, *History of the Training of Teachers in Scotland,* [Edinburgh,1970] p. 85. By the Act of 1872, the old national network was merged in a new system of public schools under popularly elected school boards and controlled by a co-ordinating central authority, the Scotch Education Department.

[28] Burns, Robert, *The Inventory,* lines 40/41.

[29] *Acts of the General Assembly of the Church of Scotland* (hereafter *Acts Gen. Ass.*), 'Pastoral Admonition' 1834 p. 2.

[30] A.A., Dailly Kirk Session Records, CH2/392/2, 7th January 1750.

[31] A.A., Kirkoswald Kirk Session Minutes, CH2/562/2, 16th June 1765.

[32] *Acts of the General Assembly of the Free Church of Scotland,* 1858, p. 182.

[33] *Acts of the General Assembly of the Free Church of Scotland,* 1862, p. 498–500.

[34] *Acts Gen Ass.,* 1869, p. 58–59.

[35] *Acts Gen Ass.,* 1861, p. 79–81.

[36] Proceedings of the General Assembly of the Free Church, 24th May 1897, p. 484.

[37] Galt, John, *The Member,* [1832; Edinburgh, 1975], p. 64–65.

[38] MacDonald, John, *Memoirs of an Eighteenth Century Footman,* [London, 1790], Beresford, John, ed., [London, 1927].

[39] A.A., Kirkmichael Kirk Session Records, CH2/1333/2.

[40] *ibid.*

[41] *ibid.*

[42] *ibid.*

[43] Story, Janet, *Early Reminiscences,* [Glasgow, 1911], p. 272.

[44] *ibid,* p. 279.

[45] *ibid,* p. 294.

[46] Story, Janet, *Later Reminiscences,* [Glasgow, 1913], p. 297–298.

[47] A.A., Ayrshire Sound Archive, ASA 077, *Life in Domestic Service.*

Chapter 2: Hiring and Firing

There were four ways in which servants might seek employment or in which employers might obtain servants. These were by word of mouth, at hiring fairs, through registries or through newspaper advertisements.

Finding a Place by Word of Mouth

The oldest of these methods is that of word of mouth. It is as old as the contract of service itself and still continues to this day. It is not possible to establish the frequency of its use but some examples are recorded.

John MacDonald, the eighteenth century footman already mentioned, used this method throughout his career in service. It would seem more than likely that servants employed by, and having direct contact with, the gentry would be recommended personally.

Correspondence in the Kennedy of Kirkmichael papers regarding a Miss Jenny Adams, a cousin of David Kennedy, the young laird of Kirkmichael House and estate, shows how difficult obtaining a situation could be. She had been employed as a governess in Berwickshire for a year before writing from Edinburgh to her impecunious cousin David for assistance. Her letter was dated 23rd December. No year was given, but other letters regarding her plight were dated 1787 and 1792. In this particular letter she wrote:

> I was at Sir Alexr Purves' in Berwick Shire a year and left it on their intending to Exchange their Governess for a Tutor to their sons – it is a very agreeable family, but as Sir Alexr is at present married to his fourth Lady & the family very numerous, my encouragement very small and not at all adequate to the trouble – indeed I have never had it in my power to save anything in any family I was in, as I found always enough to do to keep myself in decent cloaths and in the character of a Governess it is necessary to be genteelly dressed – and when leaving one family it is often a year before you can get another – by which means anything I may have got is spent – thus my Dr Cousin you see it is not choice but necessity that makes me troublesome to my relations.[1]

She, like many unfortunate women of her time, had remained unmarried, either through choice or lack of opportunity, and lacking a regular and sufficient annuity from her family was compelled to seek employment in one of the few ways open to her. As a governess, she would be in the service of her employer and legally a servant, and yet she would not have been regarded as a servant by any other members of the household staff, a most unenviable situation in which to be placed.

The Culzean household accounts record 'hired March 3d 1788 Jenny Anderson's sister, 6 years at Johnstone Burn Clever good tempered gets only £4 wages and is to leave it – the other sister to go to a Milaner – I gave Jenny 10/6 for her.' This would indicate that a member of the family might use her position to further the employment opportunities of her own siblings. The housekeeper too, on occasion had a shrewd knowledge of those hired, as for example, 'June 13th 93 Jane Anderson, £2 10 upon Condition that her mother never comes to this house and that Jane never takes an article out of the Kitchen, to get 25 shs for 6 months service.' Another servant hired with reservation was Agnes Provost; the entry recorded 'Came home June – Agnes Provost (Her Mothers Name McIntosh) to get £3 the twelve months service her Mother cheated me by giving in false representation of her service.'[2]

In her very thorough and interesting study of the itinerant Irish potato harvesters, Anne O'Dowd stated:

> Seasonal and temporary workers adopted several conventional methods of finding work such as wandering from one farm to the next in the locality visited, acting on information received from others who had worked in a certain area the previous year, and on occasion, writing to farmers who traditionally hired temporary staff each year.[3]

The *[Old] Statistical Account* for Kirkoswald refers to the

> great number of Irish vagrants and beggars who daily travel the great post road from Ayr to Port Patrick; near to which on both sides, stands the greater number of farmers' houses, which are oppressed by the importunate and violent cravings of the beggars.[4]

The Rev Mr Matthew Biggar did not specify whether these obviously unwelcome people were asking for work or alms. Symington parish had the same problem, the Rev Mr William Logan remarking in 1792, 'As the great road from Port Patrick to Glasgow, &c runs through the parish, it is infested with Irish vagrants and sturdy beggars from neighbouring towns.'[5] These sturdy beggars may well have been displaced agricultural workers in the first place, for the process of 'agricultural improvements' had by this date started in Ayrshire. Through time the surplus population was to find employment in industry, leaving a shortage of workers in the countryside, particularly at harvest time. William Aiton, in 1811, deplored the retreat from the countryside of the indigenous labourers and farm servants, and in a somewhat biased manner continued:

> Instead of these, their trusty servants, they were obliged to employ, at a high rate, *indolent Highlanders, or vagrant Irishmen;* many of them the dregs of society and trained in vicious habits. There can be no comparison between INDIGENOUS COTTAGERS and HIBERNIAN RENEGADOES,

who as well as Highlanders, are strangers to the modes of labour practised in the district.[6]

The eighteenth century kirk session records contain numerous references to individual Irishmen, but it was in the nineteenth century that gangs of 'tattie howkers' first came to work in the south Ayrshire potato fields, especially in the Girvan area, just as Anne O'Dowd described. The 1893 Report of the Royal Commission on Labour stated:

> In Ayrshire, however, a considerable proportion are still found annually, they arrive early in the year for potato planting, taking next turnip singling, then early potato lifting, and lastly the corn harvest. It is stated that they usually return to Ireland with considerable funds.[7]

When large families were the norm and workers were accommodated in small dwelling houses, it was usually necessary for older children to leave home and fend for themselves. Domestic service provided shelter, food, monetary remuneration and sometimes clothing. However inadequate these levels of support were, they were often superior to those which the servants had enjoyed in their childhood homes. In some cases the employing family provided a step on the ladder of work. In many cases, a parent must have been instrumental in obtaining a child's first situation. In 1969, Dr. John Strawhorn tape–recorded the memories of some elderly inmates of Ayr Welfare Home.[8] These included Mrs Cadbury, who left school at 12 years of age, and whose mother got her a situation as a scullery maid where she stayed for two and a half years. This may have been a fairly common occurrence, for many families would have had the financial necessity to send their children out to service when they were legally able to do so. At the same time they would want to help them over the first hurdle, that of finding their first situation.

Feeing Fairs

Fairs and markets, some dating from medieval times, were opportunities for inhabitants of a scattered rural area to trade, to seek employment or labour and to partake of the social activities on offer.

An anonymous ballad describes the Kirkdandy Fair which was held on the last Sunday in May, in the parish of Barr. According to Aiton:

> A vast collection of people still meet about Whitsunday every year, at the ruins of a popish chapel, that had been dedicated to the Holy Virgin and which was termed Kirk–Dominae, (Corrupted Cardamne) situated in the parish of Barr, in a muirish district, where there is not a single house and which is many miles from any inn, or place where victuals or lodging can be procured.[9]

In his 1925 *An Anthology of Carrick,* Malcolm Finlayson, a former Headmaster of Girvan High School, gave the words, but no tune (see Appendix 1).[10] The ballad describes the fair as seen through the eyes of a young man called Robin, or more familiarly Rab, who set out from home dressed in his ruffled shirt and Sunday coat, but casting the latter after a strenuous hill climb on the way to the fair. On arrival, he counted sixty–three tents, and heard the sound of pipes and fiddles. He saw couples sitting on a plank, drinking and feasting on cold haggis, braxy ham (the salted meat of a sheep that died of braxy – an intestinal disease), bread and cheese. He described how a man who had drunk too much provoked a fight in which a number of others joined '[t]ill some lay on the ground.' Next he tried unsuccessfully to persuade a shy lass to have a drink with him. He consoled himself with the thought that there were plenty of other pretty girls who would be less inhibited. Nevertheless, he admitted that many of the lads and lassies who came to the fair and indulged in sexual activities would perhaps be sorry for it. This was implying that a subsequent pregnancy would result in public disapproval and sanctions being taken against both parties, but particularly the girl.

Two verses of the ballad seem to sum up the reasons why people attended the fair:

> And mony a lad and lass cam' there,
> Sly looks and winks to barter.
> And some to fee for hay and hairst,
> And others for the quarter.
>
> Some did the thieving trade pursue,
> While ithers cam' to sell their woo';
> And ithers cam' to weet their mou,
> And gangs wi' lassies hame, man.

This fair acquired a reputation for fights between the indigenous population and the Irish who came from the Girvan area. As roads were improved, and with the coming of the railway, Kirkdandy Fair was superseded by Girvan Fair before it too gave way to that of Ayr. An itinerant street singer named James McCartney, quoted by the Rev. Roderick Lawson as 'the last of the ballad singers,'[11] sang about Girvan Fair that was held on the first Monday of April and October for stock, hiring servants and general business.[12] An oral–history tape records the tune of the ballad, although the singer, Mrs Garven, had difficulty in recalling the words.[13] Not only was essential business conducted at the feeing fairs, but it was a day out for the country folk for miles around. Finlayson provided a thumbnail sketch of Girvan Fair,

> Even as late as 1890, it was difficult to make one's way along the
> main street, closely packed with country lads and lassies, for whose

entertainment there were shows, hobby–horses, shooting galleries, ballad singers, fiddlers, and endless stands and stalls of 'sweeties' and cheap goods of all kinds.[14]

He also provided the words of the ballad:

> This morning I got early up,
> And shaved and caimed my hair, Sir,
> A cog o' brose I soon did sup,
> And started to the Fair, Sir,
> I filled my pouch wi' cheese and bread,
> Put in my purse a crown, Sir,
> An' aff I set wi' a' my speed,
> An' into Girvan toon, Sir.
>
> Oh, there were folk frae Ballantrae,
> An' some frae far Stranraer, Sir,
> Frae Minnibole and Colmonell,
> Kirkoswald and the Barr, Sir.
> Frae Weary Neuk and Dinnimuck,
> An' a' alang the shore, Sir,
> An' sic a crowd in Girvan toon.
> Was never seen before, Sir.
>
> There were apples, pears and juicy plums,
> Wi' nuts and raisins fine, Sir,
> An' candyrock to please young folk
> An' toys o' every kin', Sir
> The lassies a' wi' open mouths
> At ilka stan' stood starin'
> An' aye they cried to country youths,
> "Come here and buy's a fairing',"
>
> Sae, into Burn's Inn we gaed,
> An' ca'd a double gill, Sir,
> An' for a pie–the–piece we sent,
> Likewise a waugh o' yill, Sir,
> An' then we ca'd M'Cartney up
> An' he sang us "Kirkdandie"
> "That I may never sin," says Flynn,
> "That's worth a glass o' brandy,"

James T. Gray, for forty years the estate factor of the late Marquis of Ailsa and an authority on the history of Maybole wrote:

> Fairs were held in the town in the months of February, May, August and November where farm servants were fee'd and goods of every description were sold and it was at one of these fairs in 1756 that Robert Burns' father and mother met for the first time at a booth near the foot of the High Street.[15]

Illus. 7: The Feeing Fair at Cumnock (undated). (Courtesy of the Baird Institute, Cumnock)

Cumnock in the eighteenth and early nineteenth centuries held three fairs; later increased to four. Most of the feeing was arranged at the Race Fair in March that was held on the third Tuesday after Candlemas and at the Hin–hairst Fair that was held on the Wednesday after the third Tuesday of October. In addition, some harvest workers would be engaged at the Scythe Fair which took place on the Wednesday after the first Tuesday in July, and haymakers would be engaged at the May Fair which sometimes fell in early June because it was held on the Wednesday after the last Tuesday in May. Writing in 1899, the local Free Church minister, the Rev John Warrick, reckoned that over 2,000 people were attending the Race Fair and the Harvest Fair, although much of the hiring was done at registries in the town. The May Fair and the Scythe Fair had ceased to be well attended and the latter 'was given up for the first time in July, 1898.'[16]

The Hiring Fairs in Ayr were held on the third Tuesday in April and the third Tuesday in October, and in 1907, additional hiring fairs were held on the last Tuesday of May and October, presumably to cater for those who had not been able to negotiate a satisfactory deal at earlier fairs.

At the hiring fairs, shepherds could be identified by the crooks which they carried, the crafting of which could show considerable artistic skill. It is likely that some other types of servant displayed emblems to identify their particular skills and so draw the attention of masters wishing to hire servants. Certainly this was the case in other parts of the country. Thomas Hardy referred to the emblems worn by servants seeking employment at a hiring fair, where 'carters and waggoners were distinguished by having a piece of whipcord twisted round their hats; thatchers wore a fragment of woven straw, shepherds held their crooks in their hands and thus the situation required was known at a glance.'[17] In the Border country of Glendale '[t]he hinds wore a sprig of hawthorn in their hats, the carters a piece of whipcord, and the shepherds a tuft of wool, as emblems of their respective callings.'[18] In Ireland, according to Anne O'Dowd, '[a]t the hiring fairs and places the farmers recognised the labourers who were available for work by their general demeanour and dress, by their implements and belongings or by some special emblem.' She described the dress variations in various Irish localities and how Irish workers migrating to other parts of Ireland or to Great Britain carried their spare clothes in a bundle which indicated that they were seeking employment. 'Sometimes the bundle was wrapped in a red handkerchief and other times the clothes were simply wrapped in a square piece of cloth tied at the four corners.'[19]

A frequent sight in Ayrshire must have been the potato diggers who, she said, tied 'their bundles to their spades or loys (long, narrow spades with footrests) as soon as they arrived in the town on market or fair days.'[20] In Co Antrim and Co Down, from where most of the Irish migrants to south Ayrshire came, it seems that the wearing of emblems by servants seeking work was particularly prevalent. There,

> The emblem carried by those advertising that they were available for hiring was usually either a stick or a straw. The stick sometimes described as a white rod i.e. a peeled sally [willow] rod. The straw either sewn to some item of clothing, chewed in the mouth or held in the hand.[21]

Aiton wrote in 1811:

> There are some fairs in every town, and at every parish church, in the county of Ayr. There are five or six in Ayr, five in Irvine, three great, and several small ones in Kilmarnock, four in Maybole, five in Newmills, five or six in Cumnock, and no less than twelve in Mauchline every year.[22]

He had calculated that 'there are not less than 200 fairs and races in the county of Ayr, every year, and on average there cannot be fewer than 1,000 people at every fair or race.' Aiton deplored this excess and wanted the number to be reduced and confined to the larger centres of population. The problems associated with the Ayrshire feeing fairs, which were still general, were raised in the report of the 1870 Royal Commission on Agriculture. In this, it was pointed out that, 'they are gradually falling into disuse and the best ploughmen are not in the habit of frequenting them!'[23]

It seems that the farmers disliked the system and had been trying to organise a system of registration. One of the reasons given for their dislike of the system was because it was the custom for a farmer to give a servant 'arles' (an earnest; money to bind the bargain) when the deal was struck, which was generally half–a–crown. Some rogue servants took the money from the farmers and failed to appear for work.[24]

Another criticism was of the amount of alcohol that was drunk at the fairs. People in the towns thought the rural servants were intemperate people, whereas their behaviour at the fairs was not typical of their lifestyle for the rest of the year. There were those who argued that to abolish these fairs would be to deprive rural servants of their holidays. The Commissioners' answer to this was the somewhat middle class view 'that servants should have holidays with some rational entertainment.'[25]

A further problem cited was that of assessing potential servants' characters since 'servants seldom carry a written character with them and it is rarely in engaging them that there is time at the fair to search out and make inquiry at any of their previous employers.'[26] This militated against paying servants according to their merit.

Over the years, these fairs changed in character. The growth of shops and agricultural suppliers obviated the need to deal in essentials at fairs, the institution of auction marts the need to buy and sell animals at fairs, while the setting up of registries in towns gradually decreased the need for feeing deals to be made on the open street regardless of the weather.

Gradually the fairs evolved into the seasonal visits of travelling people providing entertainment, known locally as 'The Shows.' In Ayr, for example, this entertainment now coincides with the Ayr Gold Cup horse race which is held on the third weekend in September. It is a time when young people and families enjoy the thrills of the roundabouts and similar fairground amusements.

The *Third Statistical Account of Ayrshire,* published in 1951, took a retrospective look at the feeing fairs which by that time had been abolished and replaced by the Employment Exchange. Although a 'definite caste division' was discerned between farmers and farm workers, the workers had started to reappraise their status.

The farm workers don't like being called 'farm servants' or 'farm labourers' as they used to be. The first of these names signifies to them servitude from which they are striving to escape; the second suggests – wrongly – that they are unskilled workers.[27]

Nevertheless, some nostalgia was shown for the feeing fair which 'was a custom locally looked forward to every six months by the farm workers with great enthusiasm.'[28] It was an opportunity for them because '[t]here they had many social hours with their cronies and many a romance started at a fair dance.' Farm workers had very few holidays, but the fair which was held about a month before the May and November terms was recognised as such.

Employment Agencies

As has been mentioned in the previous section of this chapter, by 1870 the farmers were trying to set up registries. The Royal Commission on Agriculture that year recommended:

> Register offices, with paid registrars where servants may enter their
> names without paying a fee and give references as to character, seem to be
> the most generally approved substitution for hiring fairs.[29]

Situations in the country establishments of the gentry tended to be found in a select register located in Edinburgh. One such was used by the Hamiltons of Rozelle in the 1860s. The registry provided the potential employer with a reference. One would expect such references to have been reasonably truthful and accurate, otherwise clients would have ceased to patronise that particular registry. When a mistress considered applications for a situation in her household, she would probably consider their previous experience and make enquiries about their characters. Undated notes found in the Rozelle Papers would suggest this to be the case.

On occasion, the assistance of a reputable local retail establishment might be enlisted to find a trustworthy and competent woman to undertake unsupervised domestic tasks.

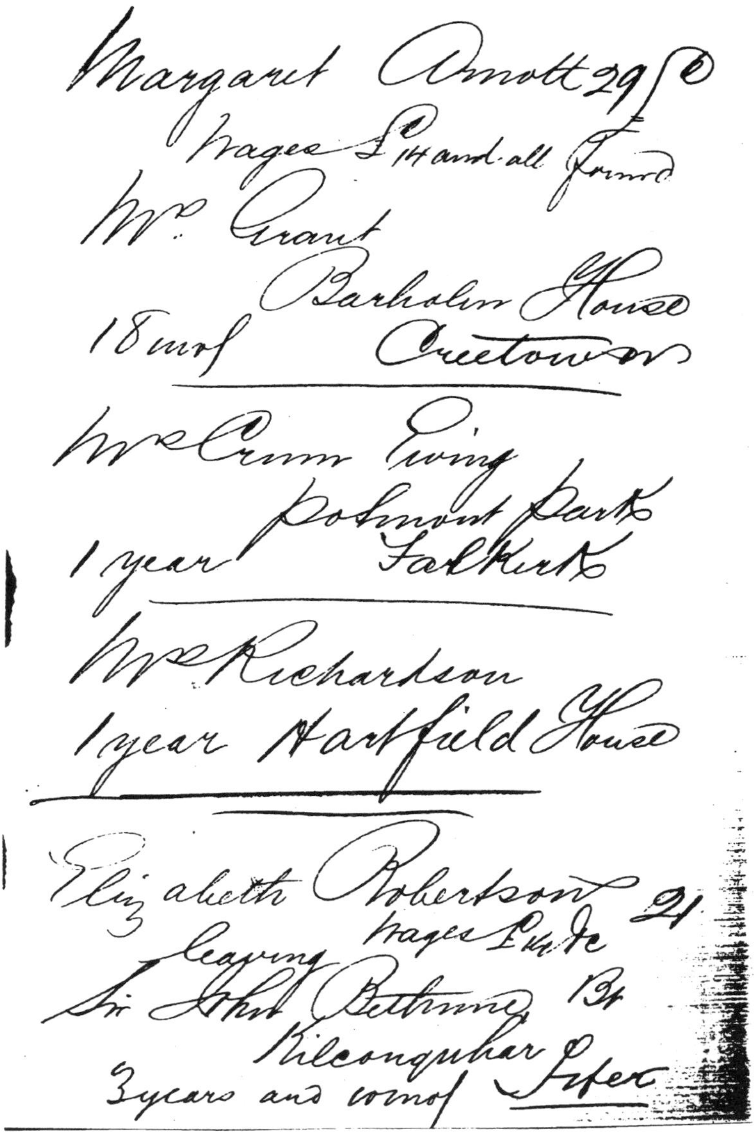

Margaret Arnott 29
Wages £14 and all found

Mrs Grant
Barholm House
18 mnf Creetown

Mrs Crum Ewing
Polmont Park
1 year Falkirk

Mrs Richardson
1 year Hartfield House

Elizabeth Robertson 21
Leaving Wages £14 &c
Sir John Bethune 134
Kilconquhar Fife
3 years and some of

Illus. 8: Notes made by a mistress of Rozelle with a vacancy in her domestic staff (undated). (Ayrshire Archives, Hamilton of Rozelle and Carcluie Papers, SAC/DC/17/27/4/1)

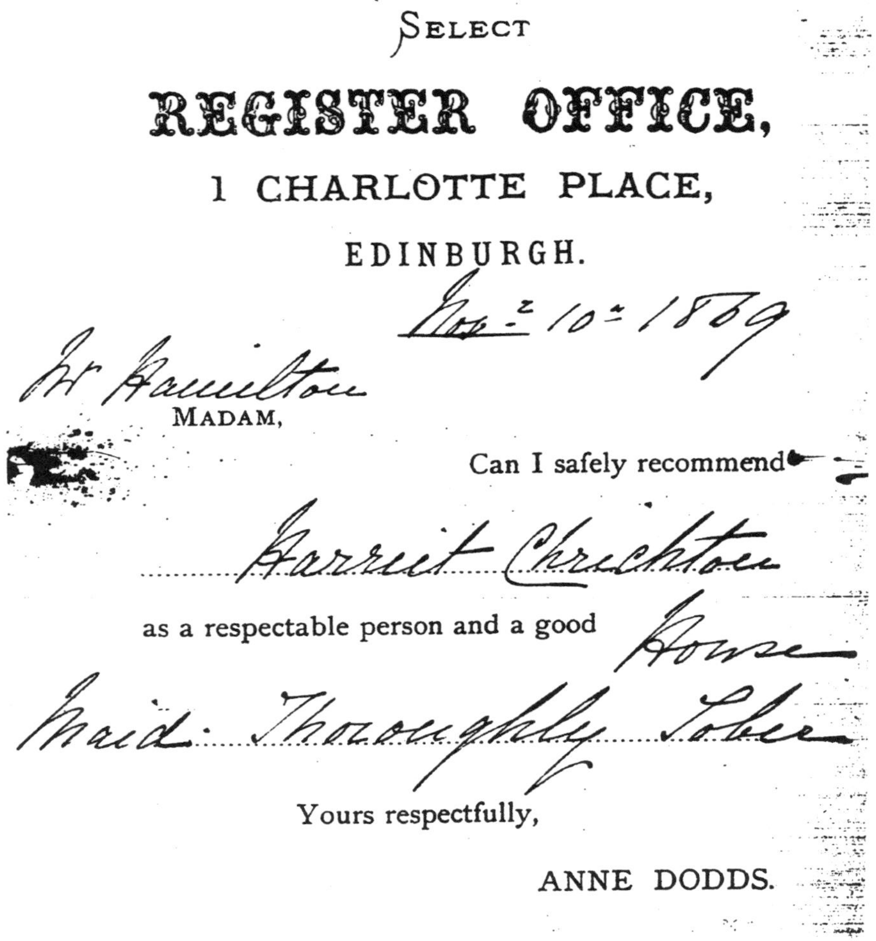

Select

REGISTER OFFICE,

1 CHARLOTTE PLACE,

EDINBURGH.

Nov 10 1869

Mr Hamilton

MADAM,

Can I safely recommend

Harriet Chrichton

as a respectable person and a good *House*

maid. Thoroughly Sober

Yours respectfully,

ANNE DODDS.

Illus. 9: A reference supplied by a Registry. (Ayrshire Archives, Hamilton of Rozelle and Carcluie Papers, SAC/DC/17/27/6/4)

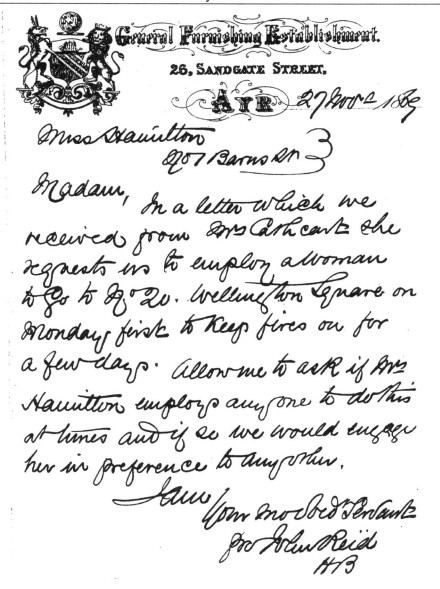

Illus. 10: Letter from the General Furnishing Establishment, Ayr (Ayrshire Archives, Hamilton of Rozelle and Carcluie Papers, SAC/DC/17/27/3/9))

Mrs Hume, formerly employed at Bargany, explained on a tape–recording how servants obtained their posts through a registry in Edinburgh called Fife's.

> You paid a yearly subscription 2/6d, then 5/– as your wages rose. When you wanted a job, you just wrote and told them you were in need of a job. You told them where you'd been for references and what your position had been if you wanted to go up a step. Mrs Sharp, the Cook/Housekeeper at Bargany spoke broad Scots to everybody. Fife was a retired butler. Ward, also a butler, succeeded him. Somebody had to recommend you. Mrs Sharp recommended me. You didn't pay money when you got the job. Fife's got jobs for people abroad.[30]

By the second half of the nineteenth century, Domestic Servant Registries were starting to be established in Ayr. One reason for this was the coming of the railway which opened up the Ayrshire coastal towns to tourists, many of whom came to follow the popular vogue for salt water bathing. A number found lodgings in the resort towns and thus created a demand for domestic staff to service their needs. The registries helped the servants to find situations and the employers to find suitable servants. They acted as a filter, saving both parties from having to experience many fruitless interviews.

The 1849–50 Trade Directory for Ayr mentions a Registry for Servants run by a Mrs Sprent, in the Kirk Port, High Street. The 1858–59 Directory, refers to her as Mrs Sprent Baird and in subsequent records she is referred to simply as Mrs Baird. Initially, she operated her business from 6 Kirk Port, then in 1873 at number 8 where she remained until 1881. Despite competition over the years, she remained in business for thirty–four years.

Her first competitor was a Mrs Corner, who operated from the Sandgate where her husband had a perfumers and hairdressing business. No doubt his customers would use his wife's registry.

From the 1870s onwards, the number of registries grew and in the period 1906–1909, there were as many as twelve operating. Thereafter they declined, leaving six in existence from 1912–1915. A number of registries only lasted a year or two, but many survived for surprisingly long periods.

James Scott began his business in 1896 at 6 New Bridge Street, transferring to 68 Newmarket Street in 1900. In 1906–07 he renamed the business Scott's Registry, and moved it to 36 Newmarket Street in 1912–13. It was still listed in the 1914–15 Directory. In addition to his registry for servants, he also had the agency for the main shipping companies and offered tickets at the lowest rates to the various colonies of the British Empire, which must have been convenient for servants wishing to emigrate.

Hunters opened in 1902–03 at 4 Sandgate, moving to 21 Sandgate in 1906–07 and it too was still listed in the 1914–15 Directory. It combined the servants' registry with a dry cleaning agency and an agency for a local cab and carriage hirer.

Mrs James Clark ran a servants' register at 80 Sandgate from 1889–93, combining it with being a coal merchant and an agent for steamers, and at the turn of the century Mrs D.C. Spencer of 82 Sandgate was an agent for the Greenan Steam Laundry and a coal merchant as well as being a registrar for servants.

Back in 1864–65, Miss Jane Wilson, who lived in 64 Sandgate, operated a fruiterers and registered office for servants, but it seems to have been a short lived business.

Miss Murdoch opened her Registry in 1870–71 at 8 Fort Street, moving to 15 Cathcart Street in 1873–74, and was listed as a mangle–keeper and registrar for servants. She was probably in a position to know the characters and capabilities of the local washerwomen and laundrymaids. In 1880–81, she moved across the bridge into Newton–upon–Ayr, being at 25 New Road in 1880–81 and 49 New Road North in 1882–83. No doubt these addresses would be more convenient for washer women, because with the very marked decline in the demand for Ayrshire whitework on which hundreds of women in this area had previously been employed, those women with domestic responsibilities would have had little choice but to wash other people's linen in order to supplement the family budget.

Miss J Goudie chose 73 Alloway Street to open her registry in 1900–01 and moved to 43 Kyle Street the following year, changing the name of the business to Goudie's Registry in 1907–08, and was still listed in the 1914–15 Directory. The location of this registry would be convenient for the farming community, being fairly near the site of the cattle mart at the time, as indeed was the Country Registry which operated at various premises in Smith Street and Kyle Street from 1906–07 to 1910–11.

A full list of the Ayr servants' registries compiled from the local trade directories is given in Appendix 2.

Newspaper Advertisements

With a few exceptions, prior to the mid nineteenth century this was not a viable or locally known method of introducing masters and servants. Newspapers were expensive, subject to tax and unlikely to be seen by servants who would not have been able to afford such a luxury, although senior servants in the big houses might have had access eventually to some discarded newspapers. Also some of the labourers, particularly women, may not have been sufficiently literate to read newspapers.

From the 1860s onwards, the situation changed. Farmers sometimes passed on newspapers to their workers.. One reported, 'I lend a daily paper to my workpeople, which they seem to take an interest in.'[31] With the increase in the number of literate people, the increase in the number of newspaper titles, and the increase in their circulation figures, more people would have access to 'Situations Vacant' advertisements. By using the columns of the newspapers, employers might hope to reach a wider audience than those registered with a particular agency or attending the local hiring fair. It was not unusual for the servant registry offices to place advertisements in the *Ayr Advertiser.*

> HOUSEMAIDS, TABLEMAIDS, COOKS and GENERAL SERVANTS Wanted at JACK'S REGISTRY, 5 Newmarket Street, Ayr.[32]

> WANTED, for a House in Town, an EXPERIENCED GENERAL SERVANT, able to Milk. Must be thoroughly trustworthy and honest. Liberal wages given to a suitable person – Apply in the first instance to W.C. CURRIE, Sandgate Street.[33]

> WANTED, for now and Term, thoroughly Experienced COOKS, HOUSEMAIDS, HOUSE and TABLEMAIDS, GENERAL and UNDER SERVANTS, Apply at once, – Mrs LAMBIE'S Registry Office (Select), 4 New Bridge Street, Ayr.[34]

An early example of the local use of newspaper advertisement to find a suitable employee was when the following advertisement appeared in 1815,

> FARM SERVANT. Wanted at Whitsunday, a middle aged careful active man of experience, who can be properly recommended for sobriety and ability, with an obliging temper. As good wages will be given, none need apply but such as answer the above description. – Apply to David Norman, son of Joseph Norman, Nursery and Seedman, Air. Air, 15th March, 1815.[35]

The following examples give some indication of the variety of advertisements including some for servants wanted in other parts of the country. This could indicate that Ayrshire produced a surplus of good quality servants, or that the areas for which servants were sought had a shortage locally.

> Wanted. A Dairymaid to go to Dumfriesshire to make Cheddar Cheese – Apply to ROBERT DRUMMOND, Bogwood, Mauchline.[36]

> WANTED for Ayr, a GOOD PLAIN COOK. Three Servants kept. Address, "120," 'Advertiser' Office.[37]

> WANTED, a WOMAN of middle age, as a General Servant, to take charge of Kirkmichael Mains. – One accustomed to Laundry Work will be preferred. – Apply to Mr GEORGE MAIR, KIRKMICHAEL LODGE, BY MAYBOLE. Kirkmichael Lodge, 6th April, 1881.[38]

COOK–GENERAL – Can any Lady recommend a good Cook–General for the Country? Address – Mrs C.P. LLOYD, Exning, Suffolk.[39]

NURSERY GOVERNESS, WANTED, Three boys; must be a good sewer and knitter. State salary, also age, to "236," 'Advertiser' Office.[40]

Servants applying for a domestic situation would normally be interviewed to ascertain their suitability for the place. In a large establishment such as Dumfries House, the house steward would engage and dismiss the servants. In the houses of the gentry such as Rozelle, it would normally be the butler who engaged the indoor male servants and the housekeeper who engaged the female servants. The master of the household would select his own valet, and the mistress her own lady's maid, nurse and cook. The master would also engage the coachman except where this task was undertaken by the steward. He would engage the grooms, too, unless the coachman was considered capable of engaging the grooms and other stable helpers. In smaller households where senior staff were not employed the mistress would have to interview potential servants herself.

Advice given in 1894 to those conducting the interview suggested that the applicant should be questioned about their current situation, the length of their service there, reason for leaving, their age, state of health, the wage they had been receiving and whether they were early risers.[41] This to be followed by questions pertaining directly to the situation for which the applicant was applying. In the case of a cook, the interviewer would seek to find out whether the applicant was a 'professed cook', how many family members and how many servants she had cooked for, whether she was used to preparing large dinners and making smart sweets and entrées. At this stage, agreement had to be reached on whether the cook could select tradesmen supplying the kitchen, place the orders, settle the accounts and be allowed the cook's percentage on these. It was recommended that the interview should conclude with the applicant being made aware of the house rules, and might include such items as whether the servant would have to pay for breakages and whether female servants would be allowed male 'followers'. Such interviews could be an ordeal both for the applicant and the inexperienced mistress.

Termination of Employment

In all probability the majority of contracts of employment in service would terminate at the term time. Then, servants who were dissatisfied with their situations would try to find places that were more congenial to them or where they could better themselves. Equally, a master or mistress might choose not to re–employ a particular servant. Employers would normally seek to inquire why a servant was given notice.

There were, nevertheless, cases in which servants had to leave their place, often abruptly. Maids who became pregnant could expect to be dismissed even if they had been violated by the master or son of the household. Such young women were fortunate if they had a family or friends to whom they could return.

Since notice of dismissal was likely to be verbal, it is difficult to find documentary evidence of individual cases. However, George Douglas Brown's novel *The House with the Green Shutters* describes two different fictitious cases of dismissal that have a ring of reality about them. In chapter IV, Gourlay, the master of the house, summarily dismisses his servant Gilmour because the latter defends himself against the impudence of the son of the house.[42] This was an ill–natured altercation between the two men, with the servant forfeiting his wages.

In marked contrast, in chapter XXII, Gourlay was obliged to dismiss his old servant Peter Riney who has served the family for fifty years. The bewildered Riney faces the prospect of ending his days in the workhouse once the few coins he has been paid are spent. For Gourlay, 'the going of Peter meant the going of everything.' For both men it was a traumatic time; as indeed it must have been for some in reality.

John MacDonald, the eighteenth century footman, provided a number of examples of hiring and firing. As referred to in the previous chapter, John Bell, the Bargany coachman, on a visit to Edinburgh hired the nine–year–old MacDonald as a postilion because he 'pleased him very well.'[43] This goodwill was not to last for, as John MacDonald matured, he often received vails that he failed to hand over to John Bell. The latter often flogged him unmercifully, sometimes till he bled, and turned him out of the stable. After six years in the Bargany service, he gave notice to his master, and when asked the reason for this he said that he was too big to ride postilion and that he wanted a coachman's place. John Hamilton offered him a post as groom, with a stable to himself, and charge of the saddle horses if he would stay. This was a tempting offer for 'it was as good as a guinea a week', but he declined it because he said, 'it would make John Bell worse against me than ever.' According to MacDonald, the parting conversation between his master and himself was as follows,

> Mr Hamilton: "Have you received any wages from me?"
>
> John MacDonald: "No sir."
>
> Mr Hamilton: "Jack, if I give you two pounds that will be enough for your pocket. Lord Crauford will give you money when you want; and I will give you a note of hand for your ten pounds, and five per cent, for it; and when you see me in Ayr, call me when the interest is due, and I will pay you."
>
> John MacDonald: "I am very much obliged to your honour . . . God Almighty bless you; and thank you for your goodness."

Despite the animosity between Bell and MacDonald, the former asked Mr Hume, the Edinburgh coachbuilder, 'if he knew of any place, for John MacDonald was about to leave Bargany service.' He further added, 'He has been postilion with us for six years since we hired him from your neighbour Mr Gibb.' Hume seemed well satisfied with this character reference and said that he had received letters 'from the Earl of Glencairn for a set of postilions, the other from the Earl of Craufurd for one to drive the postchaises and four horses, to have charge of the saddle horses, and to have a boy to assist him and to ride postilion.' He was hired to serve the Earl of Craufurd at five pounds a year, and provided with a letter from Mr Hume to take to his new master. He stayed in his post for three years, and then the earl began to take a dislike to him for some unknown reason. The relationship between them must have become difficult for John MacDonald wrote, 'Soon after the harvest of 1759, I gave my Lord warning and was discharged the fifteenth of November being Term day.' He spent the winter with his sister in Edinburgh, and learned to be a hairdresser. In 1760, Mr Hamilton, on a visit to Edinburgh asked him to dress his hair, and was so well pleased with the result that he hired John as his valet in place of James Scott who had served him for twelve years, had saved £600, and had then married the lady's maid and taken the Haugh hill farm. John served at Bargany, and travelled with Mr Hamilton, but there came the time when Mr Hamilton suspected John of improper conduct with a lady guest. The following day, Mr Hamilton, having dined and drunk very freely, asked for one of his golf clubs, which he broke in pieces over John's back saying, 'You damned scoundrel–provide yourself a place.'

Throughout the period covered by this study, the work ethic was seldom if ever questioned. People expected and needed to work for, as will be shown later, there was little support for the able–bodied unemployed

Finding work by word of mouth was a useful method when a particular post was sought or when jobs were in short supply. The hiring fair, for so long of importance to both masters and servants, gradually declined as the more efficient services provided by the servant registries and newspaper advertisements expanded.

Termination of employment was usually a time of stress. Sometimes it provided the opportunity to move into a better situation, as when a servant from one of the big houses moved to another to take up a more senior position in the household. For others it might mean going 'on the tramp' in search of work, and suffering the shame and social stigma of being unemployed.

[1] A.A., Kennedy of Kirkmichael Papers, ATD 60/9/6 & ATD 60/9/12.

[2] N.A.S., Ailsa Muniments, GD 25/9/19.

[3] O'Dowd, Anne, *Spaleens and Tattie Howkers*, [Dublin, 1991], p. 102.

[4] *[Old] Statistical Account* Kirkoswald (p. 500).

[5] *[Old] Statistical Account* Symington (p. 642).

[6] Aiton, William, *General View of Agriculture in the County of Ayr*, [Glasgow, 1811], p. 522.

[7] *Royal Commission on Labour* 1893, Vol XXXVl, para 16. 1969.

[8] A.A., Ayrshire Sound Archive, ASA018, *Memories of Ayr Welfare Home.*

[9] Aiton, William, *General View of Agriculture in the County of Ayr* [Glasgow, 1811], p. 568.

[10] Finlayson, Malcolm, J, *An Anthology of Carrick,* [Kilmarnock 1925], p. 141.

[11] *ibid*, p. 268.

[12] Pigot & Co's, *Directory of Scotland* [Ayrshire, 1837], p. 257.

[13] School of Scottish Studies, ASA154, *Memories of Rural Workers,* 1962.

[14] Finlayson, Malcolm, J. *An Anthology of Carrick,* [Kilmarnock 1925], p. 267.

[15] Gray, James, T, *Maybole, Carrick's Capital* [Alloway, 1982], p. 31.

[16] Warrick, Rev. John, *The History of Old Cumnock,* [Paisley, 1899], p. 307.

[17] Hardy, Thomas, *Far From the Madding Crowd,* 1874, quoted in Mingay, G.E. *Rural Life in Victorian England,* [Stroud, 1976], p. 72.

[18] Robson, Michael, *A Corner of the North,* [Newcastle, 1909], p. 13, quoted in Devine, T.E., ed., *Farm Servants and Labour in Lowland Scotland 1770–1914,* [Edinburgh, 1984], p. 80.

[19] O'Dowd, Anne, *Spaleens and Tattie Howkers,* [Dublin, 1991], p. 119.

[20] *ibid*, p. 121.

[21] *ibid.*

[22] Aiton, William, *General View of Agriculture in the County of Ayr,* [Glasgow, 1811] p. 569–70.

[23] *Royal Commission on the Employment of Children, Young Persons and Women in Agriculture. Fourth Report. Appendix Part I and II.* Report by J.H. Tremenheere on Dumfriesshire, Kirkcudbright–Shire, Wigtownshire and Ayrshire, 1867 [hereafter Report by J.H. Tremenheere, 1867], para. 82.

[24] *ibid*, p. 82.

[25] *ibid*, p. 83.

[26] *ibid.*

[27] Strawhorn, John & Boyd, William, eds., *The Third Statistical Account of Scotland– Ayrshire,* [Edinburgh, 1951], p. 69.

[28] *ibid.*

[29] Report by J.H. Tremenheere, 1867, p. 96. para 83.

[30] A.A., Ayrshire Sound Archive, ASA 078, *Life in Domestic Service.*

[31] Report by J.H. Tremenheere, 1867, p.211. para 8.

[32] *Ayr Advertiser,* 31st March 1881.

[33] *ibid.*

[34] *Ayr Advertiser,* 17th March 1881.

[35] *Air Advertiser,* 23rd March 1815.

[36] *Air Advertiser,* 17th March 1815.

[37] *ibid.*

[38] *Ayr Advertiser,* 7th April 1881.

[39] *Ayr Advertiser,* 19th January 1899.

[40] *Ayr Advertiser,* 9th February 1899.

[41] Anon, *The Duties of Servants,* [East Grinstead, 1894], p. 9–11.

[42] Douglas, George, *The House with the Green Shutters,* [Edinburgh, 1986].

[43] MacDonald, John, *Memoirs of an Eighteenth Century Footman,* [London, 1790], Beresford, John, ed., [London, 1927].

Chapter 3: Conditions of Service

Wages, Hours and Duties

As has been mentioned already (Chapter 1), the Justices of the Peace were required 'to fix the ordinary wages of workmen, labourers and servants' and since their records are no longer available, data pertaining to the greater part of the eighteenth century are scarce.[1]

In his *General View of Agriculture of the County of Ayr,* Aiton provided a table of the rates payable between 1720 and 1809, and it seems likely that he might have had access to the records of the local Justices.[2]

	1720			1740			1760			1780			1800			1809		
	£.	s.	d.	£.	s.	d.	£.	s.	d.	£.	s.	d.	£.	s.	d.	£.	s.	d.
Ploughman per half year, with bed and board in the family,	1	0	0	1	15	0	2	10	0	4	0	0	9	0	0	12	0	0
Do. of inferior merit,	0	10	0	1	0	0	1	10	0	2	10	0	6	0	0	9	0	0
Best dairy or servant maid,	0	8	4	0	15	0	1	0	0	1	10	0	3	0	0	5	0	0
Inferior do.	0	6	0	0	12	0	0	16	0	1	0	0	2	0	0	3	0	0
Herd,	0	4	0	0	6	0	0	12	0	0	18	0	1	10	0	2	0	0
Reapers men, for 5 or 6 weeks, harvest work,	0	6	0	0	10	0	0	15	0	1	1	0	2	15	0	3	10	0
Do. Women,	0	4	6	0	7	6	0	11	0	0	16	0	2	2	0	2	10	0
Taylors, per day, with food in the family,	0	0	2	0	0	3	0	0	4	0	0	9	0	1	6	0	2	6
Masons and Wrights, with do.	0	0	4	0	0	7	0	1	0	0	1	8	0	2	6	0	3	0
Common Labourers, per day, without food, Men,	0	0	3	0	0	5	0	0	8	0	1	0	0	1	8	0	2	6
Do. do. do. Women,	0	0	2	0	0	3	0	0	6	0	0	9	0	1	0	0	1	6
Mower, Thatcher, Carpenter, or Shoe-maker, with food, per day,	0	0	2½	0	0	4	0	0	7	0	1	2	0	1	6	0	2	0

Illus. 11: Extract from Aiton's *General View of Agriculture in the County of Ayr*, 1811.

Between 1791 and 1799, the ministers of the established Church contributed to the *[Old] Statistical Account of Scotland.* A similar exercise was undertaken in the 1840s, when the *New Statistical Account of Scotland* was produced. Both collections, now available on the Internet (http://edina.ac.uk/Stat Acc/), provide a wealth of information on a wide variety of topics including, for some parishes, the prevailing wage rates (see Appendix 4).

The rates quoted in the *[Old] Statistical Account* show some variation between parishes, so it is possible that there were similar variations earlier in the century, and that Aiton's figures were averages for the county, as might be those provided by Fullarton.[3] The latter, writing in 1793, gave the rate for farm servants boarded in the family as £5 per half year, and for women servants £4–£5 yearly although this was paid half yearly. Other farm servants received £5 per half year together with 2 pecks of oatmeal, plus 6d per week maintenance. Labourers earned 12d–14d per day, but had to pay 20/–, 30/– or 40/– per annum for a small house, a garden, grass for a cow and sufficient ground for growing potatoes. When the market prices of commodities were high in relation to wage levels, it was an advantage for servants to receive part of their wages in kind.

The figures for Sorn for 1790 and 1796 in the *[Old] Statistical Account* show how rapidly wages were rising during this period of European conflict. However, rather than the manpower requirements of the army and navy, the cause was probably the growth of the cotton spinning mill in the parish at Catrine. Complaints about the rising wage levels for common labour and domestic service were expressed in the 1792 report for Dailly. In Old Cumnock, domestic servants were paid nearly the same as farm servants. The rate paid to a day labourer in Ayr might indicate that work was not guaranteed for the whole year. In Muirkirk, where male labour could be employed in both the iron and coal–tar works, this was reflected in the higher 1792–1793 rates for male workers but not for female servants, there being no apparent competition for their labour. On the other hand, rates paid to male servants in the parish of St. Quivox reflects the influx of labourers into the Wallacetown area of the parish, who even at these rates could earn more money than they could in Ireland or the West Highlands. Female rates were not lowered, there being the possibility of seeking work in the adjacent burgh of Ayr.

In the parish of Kirkoswald, comprising largely Culzean/Cassillis estate land, much of the work was done by cottagers, or work was contracted out to jobbing workers. The Ailsa Muniments provide information on the wages paid to estate workers. From 1770–1771, the four assistant gardeners were each paid £3 plus 6d per week kitchen money (an allowance in lieu of food), and 3s 6d per year for washing, making a total of £4 9s 6d per annum. Also, one labourer worked 36 days at 8d per day, and a second 232 days at 8d per day, and 78 days at 7d per day. On the Culzean home farm at the same time, day labourers were paid 8d per day, and 15d per day mowing hay, whilst one man earned 10d per day for 51 days raising stones for the road. The greatest number of days worked was 292, the majority less, and six of them had 10 shillings deducted for their cow's grass. The women only worked at harvest time and were paid 6d per day.[4]

The household accounts for Culzean, probably kept by the housekeeper, not only list the wages given, but provide interesting comments, the following being examples:[5]

> May 1766, Langton Lass to get 20sh & half a crown or 3sh for shoes or apron if She behave well to have Charge of the Dairy Milk Cows, wash an Dress or spin or Do What ever she has time for

> Nov 16 1784, John Wilson to get £6 if he behaves well to get something at the genl Assembly or to be made a footman from month to month — a month's wages or a month's warning. £6

May 21 1787, Pedry refused to go to the Cows — Constantly for which give her no present. £2

June 13th 1793, Jane Anderson, upon Condition her mother never comes to this house, and that Jane never takes an article out of the kitchen, to get 25sh for 6 months service. £2 10s.

Feb 24th 1795, Betty Ribison a months trial and if she stays to get £3

Nov 13th, to Betty Ribison Hen Wife to get & to Eat with the Maids £3

Evidence that wages eventually followed prices and started to fall after the Napoleonic Wars is shown in the 1837 *New Statistical Account* for Girvan which quoted male servants earning £14–£16 with bed and board, whereas 15–20 years before they had been earning £20. Lads able to do men's work could earn £9–£12, which raises the possibility of them having been employed in preference to older workers in order to reduce wage costs. Girls fit to manage a dairy were paid £8, whereas house servants in town earned from £4–£7, thus reflecting the greater skill and harder work expected from a dairymaid. Shearers earned 1/6d a day without victuals, although if bad weather threatened, they could earn 2s–2/6d a day, but this was rare. According to the report, the reason rates of pay were 'fully as low here as in most parts of the country, seems to be, that a great many of the cotton weavers prefer a few days in the reaping–field, to their ordinary airless and sedentary occupation.' In the upland parish of Barr, where fewer workers were required on the enlarged farms, the Poor Law Inquiry revealed 'wages have fallen.'[6]

In Straiton, the *New Statistical Account* report stated that 'There has been a more than usual demand for female servants, in consequence of the number who have lately become Ayrshire needle–workers.' Expert sewers could earn 1s a day, and although this fine work could seriously strain eye–sight, for many it would have been a preferable occupation to farm or domestic service.

An article which appeared in the *Ayr Advertiser* on 6th March 1879 provides an interesting comparison of wages and prices prevailing in the years 1832 and 1877.[7]

THE WAGES OF COTMEN PAST AND PRESENT.—A correspondent, who can speak from a good deal of personal knowledge, supplies us with a comparison of the wages of cotmen as they were in the year 1832, to which period his knowledge extends, and the year 1877. The money wages in 1832 were from £14 to £18—say, £18, besides which there would be an allowance of 6½ bolls of oatmeal at 17s 4d a boll; six bolls of potatoes at 8s; 40 creels of coals (with cartage), £1 17s 6d; free house, £2—making a total of £29 18s 2d, or about 11s 6d a week. Out of his money wage he would have to buy—say, 52lbs butter at 8d; 4 stones cheese at 7s, and 26 doz. eggs at 6d—or in all, £3 15s 8d. This would leave a balance of £14 4s 4d a year to provide clothes, schooling, butcher meat, &c. A little money was generally added—say, 50s—by the wife and members of family in harvesting. In 1877, the rate of wages was from £32 to £36—say, £36, in addition to which, there would be 10 bolls of oatmeal at £1 per boll; free house, £2 10s; cartage of coal—say, 18s—in all, £49 8s, or 19s a week. Out of his money wage he would have to buy—say, 52lbs of butter at 1s 6d a lb; 4 stones of cheese at 14s a stone, and 26 doz. eggs at 1s—in all, £8—leaving £38 for the purposes mentioned before. This comparison brings out that the cotman was fully £18 a year better in 1877 than he was in 1832. Unmarried ploughmen in 1832 received from £4 to £7 a half year, with bed, board, and washing; while in 1877 they got from £14 to £16 in the half year, with bed and board, but no washing.

Illus. 12: Ayr Advertiser, 6th March 1879.

By 1893–94, married ploughmen could expect to earn £35 per annum, paid at the rate of 13s to 14s a week, and to be provided with a free house and a garden valued about £4 and 10 bolls of meal and flour valued at £7 10s, making a total of £46 10s, to which should be added £1 10s for carting of coals. Alternatively, some were paid at 18s per week and supplied only with a free house and a carting of coals, valued at £46 16s, plus £4, a total of £50 16s. Benefits in kind could include potatoes, but milk was supplied at farm cost. Labourers' wives could earn from £4–£12 a year for occasional work. Shepherds were paid on similar terms to ploughmen. Young male farm servants could earn from £13–£16 per half year with bed and board valued perhaps 8s to 9s per week.[8]

Male labourers were employed at 15s–18s a week, and women assisting with milking could earn 1s a day or in some cases as little as 3s 6d a week. Female farm servants were paid £9–£11 per half year with bed and board. Female field workers' daily rates of pay ranged from 1/3d in winter to 1/6d in summer. Some women combined milking and field work, the former being considered heavy work. At harvest time, women, other than regular servants employed for the term, could earn 3s to 3s 6d a day.[9]

One of the issues covered by the Royal Commission on Labour of 1893–94, concerned the hours worked by the various categories of agricultural workers, and in all probability they would not have been less in earlier years. Ploughmen and others engaged with draught animals were expected to start work in the stable at 5 a.m. or 5.30 a.m. at all times of the year, to feed the horses, clean the stables and prepare the food for later in the day. After breakfast, they started work in the fields at 7 a.m. in the summer and as soon as it was light in winter. At noon, there was a break for dinner, then work again until 6 p.m. or until darkness fell in winter, when a further 30 to 45 minutes was spent on stable work before taking it in turns to return to the stable at 8 p.m. to check the horses. Cattlemen worked from 5 a.m. to 6 p.m. or later both summer and winter. Day labourers and women working in the fields laboured from 7 a.m. to 6 p.m. in summer and from daylight to dark in winter. Dairywomen started milking about 4 a.m., sometimes as early as 3 a.m. and certainly before 5 a.m. throughout the year. Thereafter, they had to perform domestic duties, often until 8 p.m., although there could be a slack period in the afternoon, especially in winter.[10]

In the houses of the aristocracy and the gentry, duties were very specifically designated to the various grades of servant, and although the younger members of staff may have found some of the tasks arduous at times, there were opportunities for promotion to a more senior position with possibly more congenial duties to perform. This was seldom the case with the general servant or maid–of–all–work who was employed by less affluent families.

She had to rise early to light the fire to boil water, after she had emptied the ashes and cleaned the grate and hearth. Then she had to clean the parlour, including the fireplace. This involved protecting the hearth rug and carpet, raking and removing the ashes, brushing up the dust, cleaning and polishing the grate and fireirons, blackleading the sides and rear of the hearth, setting the fire and finally washing the marble hearth. The carpet then had to be brushed and the furniture dusted and polished, so that the room was ready for the employing family to have breakfast. Next, the passage or lobby and the front steps had to be cleaned and the brass knocker polished. When she had served the family breakfast, she had to empty the bedroom slop–pails, refill the water–ewers, clean the bedroom fireplaces, air and make the beds, sweep the carpet, rugs and floor surround, dust and polish the furniture. Throughout the day the coal scuttles had to be replenished, dishes and kitchen utensils washed and dried, knives and boots cleaned, the table set and cleared, the kitchen kept clean and tidy, water fetched from the pump, oil lamps filled and wicks trimmed. There would be food to prepare and sometimes children to help dress. Laundry was not undertaken by a washerwoman, this could add to the servant's duties. Often wash day would entail carrying water from the well, pump or water butt, filling the copper boiler and lighting the fire under it to heat the water, scrubbing the clothes and rinsing them in tubs, wringing them out possibly with the help of a mangle, drying the clothes and ironing them with flat irons. House cleaning was a constant chore and particularly so on Saturdays when the house had to be prepared for the Sabbath when work was supposed to be kept to a minimum. Often it would be 11 p.m. before the poor girl was free to go to bed for a few brief hours before starting the endless round of duties again. It would appear that usually the duties required of this type of servant were numerous and onerous and for the most part at the whim of the employer.

Accommodation

The majority of servants in south Ayrshire were provided with bed and board on the farms in which they served. Writing in 1811, Aiton reported how common it was for both men and maid servants to sleep in the farm kitchen, where food was prepared and eaten, cheese was made, and dairy operations frequently undertaken. He criticised the amount of space occupied by the beds and the inconvenience this would be to the girls working in the kitchen. He was also of the opinion that it was unhealthy for people to sleep on the ground floor, particularly since the floor was 'composed of damp clay and the atmosphere moist.'[11] Expressing his moral indignation he condemned the lack of privacy afforded in the farmhouses where the male and female servants slept, dressed and undressed in the same communal apartment. He found it surprising that this practice was permitted by the ministers and elders who were usually held to be 'the guardians of chastity and decorum,' and zealous in their efforts to detect, investigate and punish scandalous behaviour by a public shaming on the *stool of repentance*. In his opinion, these indecent sleeping arrangements should have been condemned from the pulpits. Instead, he found that, 'the servants and children of the greater part of the elders, sleep every night in that promiscuous and indelicate manner.'

Fifty years after this, the General Assembly of the Church of Scotland received its 'Report on the Increase of Immorality in the Rural Districts', and was persuaded that, 'their representations being abundantly confirmed by other evidence, [they] are constrained with grief to acknowledge that those evils had not been exaggerated; but that, on the contrary, the truth is even worse than the rumour.'[12]   As a consequence of these findings, the Assembly advocated that landed proprietors, farmers, and all other country residents employing servants had a duty to consider the accommodation which they provided for their workers. They were also exhorted to provide 'a kindly superintendence over the young of both sexes.' This supervision was to be exercised at all times so 'that opportunities for loose conversation and other temptations to sin shall be, as far as possible removed.'

Aiton's report referred to the 'considerable number of cot–houses' associated with farms which existed in the mid eighteenth century. They were usually irregular structures attached to the end of farm house or offices, 'and were generally inhabited by people in extreme indigence.' They measured about 12 or 13 square feet, had a damp floor, and lacked partitions, inner–doors, smoke funnels, glass in the window, and decent furniture. They were inhabited by 'people who were reduced to abject poverty and wretchedness,' often a single woman no longer fit to work on the farm.[13]

The 1867 'Report on the Employment of Children, Young Persons & Women in Agriculture' condemned 'the inadequate supply of cottages for the agricultural labouring class and their deplorable condition . . .'[14] It continued, 'in no county in Scotland can the want and comfort of the rural population be more disregarded. Not only are cottages not built, but the old ones are permitted to fall into decay and ruin, and no disposition is shown to replace them.' Tenant farmers frequently complained about this scarcity of cottages because it meant they had to employ unmarried men and give them board and lodging in their own houses. This lack of cottage accommodation meant the farm workers were unable to marry and may have resulted in 'an amount of immorality and illegitimacy.' Where cottages did exist they 'have seldom more than one room, in which a man, his wife and seven or eight children with the father and mother occupying one bed and the older children sleeping promiscuously in the other.'

On the Culzean estate, some people lived in disused dog kennels converted for their use. They were described as 'wretched places' where in some cases 10 or 11 persons lived in one room. The floors were of damp, broken clay and were covered with beds. The decaying thatched roofs were 'pervious to the rain which in some cottages is kept out by guano bags stretched across the rafters.'   A prominent tenant farmer on the estate disclosed how he always felt ashamed and humiliated at having to offer such accommodation to his ploughmen.[15]   The provision of buildings, including cottages for farm servants, was the responsibility of the landowner, not the tenant farmer. The report gave credit to the few good cottages erected near Culzean Castle, but commented 'the great body of landed proprietors in this county have not yet realised the importance to their own interests of providing suitable residences for the people by whom they are surrounded.' Single ploughmen at this time could be lodged in attics, often poorly lit and lacking ventilation, or they could be expected to sleep in harness or storerooms, or the stable loft. Generally, there was now segregation of the sexes, although this was not always the case in the small farm–houses. The report acknowledged the convenience of having the byre adjoining the kitchen, but criticised the practice on grounds of health and comfort.

To the 1893 Royal Commission on Labour '[t]he medical officer of health for Ayrshire stated that he had obtained the passing of a bye–law in his district against the lofts above byres as sleeping–places.'[16]

In comparison with the accommodation available to the agricultural servants, and the homes in which many of the servant class were reared, those who served in the houses of the gentry were more fortunate. When Lady Cathcart died in 1817, the contents of Rozelle House on the outskirts of Ayr were auctioned. The inventory prepared for the auction gives an indication of the furnishings of various rooms, although it must be accepted that in order to facilitate house the sale, items may have been moved from their normal position in the house.[17]

The Servants' Hall contained a table, chairs and benches, 3 voiders (trays), a copper coal scuttle, irons etc., tin water pitchers, a tin flagon, 2 cans, a lanthorn, tongs, poker and 10 knives and forks. These were all sold for £3 16s 6d.

In the Butler's Room were 3 tent beds, 3 feather beds, 3 bolsters, a pillow, curtains, 4 pair of blankets for the first bed and blankets for the other two. Either the Butler shared his room with visiting valets, or the extra beds had been moved into his room for the convenience of the sale. The contents raised £14 10s. The Butler's Pantry held a press, 2 chairs and a basin stand. All sold for £1 6s 6d.

The Housekeeper's Room contained a bedstead and curtains, feather bed bolster and pillows, 3 blankets and binder, a carpet and hearth rug, 5 chairs, 4 tables, a chest of drawers, 2 presses, a cupboard, a small looking glass, 3 tea trays, a server, breadbasket, spoon tray, small beam scales and weights, 4 teapots, 3 pairs brass candlesticks, a quantity of stoneware and cans, a Carron gate, fender, irons & hearth brush.

It would appear that this room served both as a sleeping quarters and a working headquarters for the housekeeper. The contents raised £12 4s 6d.

Contrastingly, the contents of the Women's Sleeping Room raised only £6 16s 3d for 2 bedsteads, a tent bed and curtains, 4 chaff ticks (mattress ticking filled with chaff removed from threshed corn) & 3 feather bolsters, a parcel of feathers, 11 pairs of Scotch blankets & 3 stoups. There seems to have been no provision made for the storage of the women's clothes etc. or a mirror, floor covering or fireplace. No doubt the servants would provide their own box or trunk to hold their personal possessions.

In the Footman's Room were 2 feather beds, 2 pillows, 4½ pairs Scotch blankets and covers, a chair and stand, total value, £8 12s 9d.

The Stable Loft held 2 chaff beds and bolsters, 6 pairs blankets and covers, worth £3 1s in total.

The contents of Lady Cathcart's own bedroom seem to have been sufficient for her personal maid to share her room and be on hand to provide care and attention to the elderly lady at night if required.

One of the purchasers at the sale was Mrs. Miller, the cook, who bought the bedstead and bedding in the small white bedroom, and another was John Anderson, the coachman, who bought the tent bed and curtains.

When Lady Cathcart's niece, Lady Jane Montgomery, married and made her home at Rozelle, the building was upgraded and new furnishings provided. Her husband, Archibald Hamilton, made a meticulous inventory of the contents in 1845.[18]

The lady's maid now had a very comfortable room, with 2 bedsteads and curtains, 2 straw mattresses, 2 hair mattresses, 2 feather bolsters, 3 feather pillows, 2 binder blankets, 3 pairs English blankets, 2 covers, a carpet and hearth rug, fender & fire irons, chest of drawers, dressing table & glass, work table, wash hand stand, basin and ewer with a broken mouth, soap dish, pots, pails etc, 3 chairs, a stool, coal box & broom, 9 named pictures & 2 Chinese boxes.

The housekeeper now had two rooms, a bedroom with similar furnishings to that of the lady's maid, and a sitting room with a couch, arm chairs, mahogany tables & foot stool etc.

The Women's double bedroom still did not have a floor covering, but it did have window and bed curtains, a dressing table & mirror, a chest of drawers and storage trunk. The beds and bedding were well provided, although the blankets were Scotch, rather than English Witney blankets used by the upper servants and Lady Jane herself. There was a broken fender and tongs, so a fire must have been possible. The mouth of the ewer was broken, the handles were off the chamber pots, and the panes of glass were cracked and broken in the bedroom and in the passage.

The cook had a separate bedroom, apparently without floor coverings or fire, and again the ewer mouth was broken and the chamber pot chipped.

A second women's double bedroom did have some sort of carpet and a fireplace, but both the chamber pots had their handles off and one was chipped, and a pane of glass was broken and cracked. It would be interesting to know whether the servants at Rozelle were careless with the furnishings in their quarters or whether items which became chipped or cracked in the main part of the house were relegated for use by the servants.

In 1905–06, the architect Robert Weir Schulz was preparing plans for alterations to Dumfries House, home of the Marquess of Bute, where money was probably not a problem. These included a screen in the servants' bathroom and a new upper servants' bathroom.[19]

The maid–of–all–work in Ayr and the other towns was probably expected to accept very basic accommodation in the home of her employer.

The differences in accommodation and furnishing provided illustrate one aspect of the class system whereby the higher one's standing on the social scale, the better the level of comfort provided. In general, over time, conditions did improve somewhat for all, though not without considerable effort being made to change the attitude of many masters and landowners.

Food and Drink

The production, preparation and consumption of food were of prime importance to the servant class of this area as of most others throughout Scotland. Farm servants and labourers and estate gardeners toiled long hours to produce the food for home consumption and the market. The kitchen staff of the gentry and the women of the farms prepared the food and all had an interest in consuming enough to sustain the hard physical labour which was their daily lot.

Elizabeth Mure, who lived on the Caldwell estate in Renfrewshire and north Ayrshire, wrote an account of life as she recalled it between 1727 and the 1760s:

> The servants eat ill; having sett form for the week, of three days broth and salt meat, the rest meagre with plenty of bread and small beer . . .[20]

In south Ayrshire, the fare was probably poorer still. Prefixed to *The Modern Farmers' Guide* and written by 'A Real Farmer' is an account of his life and travels in Ireland, Scotland, England and America. He observed:

> From Stranraer to within five or six miles of Ayr . . . Labour here is also below par, having nothing to do but sleep, Oat–meal and milk is their chief living . . . They import into Ayr and Glasgow much corn from Ireland, particularly oats and oatmeal. There is a great consumption here of those articles, as the common people's living is chiefly oat–bread and grewel porridge or soup.[21]

Henry Graham cited an English traveller in Scotland who commented in 1766:

> The food of the farmers and workers was monotonously poor, for they had nothing to eat except the everlasting oatmeal and 'knockit bere', and kail greens from the yards – for other vegetables were almost unknown to them; beef and mutton they never tasted, unless a cow or sheep was found dead of disease, old age or hunger.[22]

Some servants had access to tea even in the eighteenth century. Mary Dall was employed at Culzean in 1798, at a wage of £4 and for tea £1 1s.[23]

In John Galt's *Annals of the Parish*, the fictitious Rev. Micah Balwhidder encountered in 1761 three or four elderly women taking tea, probably laced with cognac, behind a hedge. As he explained, 'they made their tea for common in the pint–stoup, and drank it out of caps and luggies, for there were but few among them that had cups and saucers.'[24] Since smuggling was rife along the Ayrshire coast at this time, both tea and brandy would be available to the many who in one way or another aided the illicit trade.

The Agricultural Revolution occurred later in Ayrshire than in the east of the country, but by 1811 William Aiton was able to report that 'the food and mode of living . . . of the farmers, and their servants and labourers, are more comfortable than what are enjoyed by those of their rank in any other part of Scotland.'[25] He amplified this observation with specific details of the food with which the servants of farmers of all ranks were provided, viz,

> . . . for *breakfast,* abundance of good pottage made with whey, during eight or nine months, and with water during the rest of the year, always taken with plenty of milk, and either cheese or herrings with oat–meal cakes, or milk with cakes, or frequently both cheese and milk with bread after the porridge. For *dinner*, they are allowed, at least three or four times every week, good, substantial broth, made thick with barley, pease, beans, and garden–stuffs, with abundance of beef or mutton boiled in the broth, and eaten after them with potatoes or bread; and after the meat, as much oat–cakes and milk, or potatoes and meat as they are able to eat. Part of the broth are reserved for next day, and if there is no cold beef or mutton, every one is allowed as much cheese or fish, as they can eat, with plenty of milk and potatoes, or oat–cakes to complete the meal. Sometimes, instead of broth, potatoes are stewed with beef, mutton, or butter, and at other times, the potatoes, being divested of their skins before – are boiled, are beated into paste, mixed with a small quantity of good salt butter, and as much sweet–milk, as render them palatable food. When eaten in that state to dinner, first cheese or fish with potatoes, or oatcakes with milk and cakes are served up to crown the rustic board.

> The *supper* . . . is nine times out of ten, composed of either pottage and milk; or potatoes beaten with butter and milk . . .

> Some of the poorest and most niggardly may allow, at times, potatoes to be eaten with milk for supper; but such suppers are not commonly given to servants in Ayrshire.

> In harvest the reapers are generally allowed as many oat–meal cakes, and milk after their pottage, sowens [a dish made from oat husks and fine

meal steeped in water for a week; also sowans] or beaten potatoes at supper, as they can eat.

I have quoted from Aiton at length, because he describes so well how the simple, plentiful, home produced, yet nutritious food was served to the farm servants at that time. This may not have been the case a few years later, when the Napoleonic War was over, labour was plentiful and the price of meal was rising to the extent that the meal mill in Ayr was attacked.[26]

Aiton's report was a general one for the whole county of Ayr but there must have been local variations.

Prior to the enactment of the 1844 Poor Law, the parish ministers throughout Scotland submitted answers to a questionnaire. The answers to question 19, 'On what articles of food do the labouring classes of your parish principally subsist?' provided considerable data, although the return for Ballantrae left this question unanswered. In Coylton, both oatmeal and peasemeal were eaten. The meal in Dailly was made into potage and oatcakes. Although not stated, it is probable that this also happened in other parishes.

As could be expected, fish was available in Ayr, Newton–upon–Ayr, Dundonald parish which included the port of Troon, and Maybole parish which included the small fishing port of Dunure. It is perhaps more surprising that herring was occasionally available in Dalrymple, but no doubt when a glut of fish was landed, an enterprising trader might have found it worthwhile to transport surplus stock to this inland village.

In eleven of the parishes, milk was consumed and in Dalrymple buttermilk, so possibly the milk in some of the aforementioned eleven was also buttermilk rather than sweet milk. In Monkton, which includes Prestwick, unspecified dairy produce was available. Cheese was provided in Dalmellington, Dalrymple, Coylton, Symington and occasionally in St. Quivox and Sorn. Butter was provided in Coylton and Symington and occasionally in St. Quivox. It would appear that the provision of dairy products was largely confined to the parishes where dairy farms predominated and where not all the cheeses made were marketed.

In Stair there were 'not many families who cannot produce some butcher meat.' It was also available in Muirkirk. However, in Colmonell, Dalmellington, Mauchline and Maybole, it was only occasionally provided, as was 'animal food' in Monkton and Sorn. Pork was eaten in Barr, Dalrymple, Dundonald and occasionally in St. Quivox. Bacon was eaten in Straiton, and ham in Auchinleck, whilst in Coylton 'some few make out to keep a pig and get a little bacon and ham.' In all probability the pork, bacon and ham were all derived from the family pig.

'In Maybole, tea is generally found at the tables of the married, once a day at least', and in St. Quivox 'the women use tea generally', whilst in Stair, 'tea is understood to be in general use.' Tea and sugar were available in Straiton.

Exceptionally, loaf bread was eaten in Muirkirk where the iron–works employed most of the male population. This was probably because these workers did not receive meal as part of their wages for their oatcakes or scones to be baked at home on a girdle over an open fire. Instead they would buy oven–baked bread baked commercially.

No mention was made of fruit or vegetables, but in all probability, the kail yard and the hedgerow could provide, in season, a meagre supplement to this somewhat monotonous, though healthy, diet of meal and potatoes. It is possible that very occasionally a fresh water fish guddled in the burn, a rabbit or even a game bird caught in a poacher's snare, found its way into the diet of the poor, but information regarding such illegal treats would not have been divulged to an authority figure such as a parish minister.

Mrs Hume recalled that when she was in service, a twenty–two pound roast was left hanging over the fire for the servants and another for the dining room. Two or three chickens and a pudding also hung on the spit which was worked with a wheel and chains; the meat had to be basted regularly. Yorkshire pudding and soup had also to be made before the cook went to the church. The servants had soup only on Sunday and on one other day in the week. In winter each servant was given a plum pudding, and in summer a raspberry and redcurrant tart. At Christmas, every estate worker received a plum pudding and either a big cake of shortbread or a big mince pie. Of Christmas Day Mrs Hume said, 'You had your Christmas Dinner at midday, then the toffs had theirs in the evening. We always had turkey.'[27]

Mrs Ferguson, who had been a lady's maid, remembered how all the servants took their midday meal together in the servants' hall except for pudding. She had her dinner, tea, supper and the lunch pudding in the steward's room. The housemen took their pudding in their own sitting room, and where the laundry maids took theirs varied in different houses. The kitchen staff had their meals in the kitchen or in a wee room or scullery. The head nurse ate in the steward's room or in the nursery. Grace was said before the meal, then the butler served the ladies' maids and valets, and the first footman served the rest, so the maids were served later.[28]

These two recordings were made in 1984, when Mrs Hume was 96 years old, and Mrs Ferguson was 95 years old, so they would have been remembering domestic life in the 'big house' before the First World War. Obviously one of the advantages to be gained from service in such an establishment was a more varied diet than was available to the majority of the servant class.

Clothing

In the royal burgh of Ayr, the council in the seventeenth century was concerned with the dress of female domestic servants, and a statute of very specific requirements was enacted. This was researched by Mr. D. Murray Lyon and his unpublished notes were printed under the title of *Ayr in the Olden Times* in the local newspaper in 1875. It seemed that unmarried women of easy virtue, 'spilt women', had been appearing in public dressed in the style normally adopted by married women. The local establishment, comprising of provost, baillies, council and kirk session, took exception to this display of feminine freedom of expression. They therefore ordained that all such women, nurses and servants should henceforward dress in the manner appropriate to their status. The penalty for failing to wear a servant's cap, 'curcheyis wt hingand doon lappis', was eight days imprisonment in the black hole of the tolbooth.[29]

An Act of the Parliaments of Scotland in 1621 required '[s]ervants only to wear cloth made in the country, they may however, wear their masters' old clothes.'[30] Servants did not always wish to wear their masters' old clothes; the Culzean account book for 1783–1798 records:

> Dec 84 gave Pegie 5sh wages the last half year 2/6. N.B. She refused a gown worth 10sh.

> May 19 94 Babie Lumsden a Cloke 10sh she would not take. £3.[31]

T. C. Smout describes the dress of the seventeenth century lowland peasant as consisting of 'a plaid usually worn with trousers', and for peasant women, 'linen skirts, with a plaid draped over their heads, pinned across their bosom and falling to their knees. They were not allowed by the sessions to wear plaids in church, as this was too conductive of sleep.'[32]

The clothing worn a century later seems to have been little changed, for the Rev. John Mitchell, minister of Beith in north Ayrshire, wrote in 1780 that it was customary for the common people, both male and female, to wear a type of linen called *harn*. This was made from tow, which was 'the coarser part of the flax thrown off when it passed through the hackle', or heckle (flax–comb). After the tow had been spun and crudely bleached at home, the thread would be woven and fashioned into a hardwearing garment. A locally made flannel called plaiding was also worn.[33]

A particular instance of a plaid being worn occurred in evidence given before Kirkoswald Kirk Session on 25th April 1779, which was recorded as 'he saw the accuser and one Hugh Hogg . . . walking from Daillylung towards his house, and the man was walking under her plaid tho' it was a fair Summer Day . . .'[34] Obviously the witness did not think it unusual for a plaid to be worn, only that it was being shared on 'a fair Summer Day.'

Mitchell remarked upon the lack of attention paid to personal cleanliness at that time.[35] However, when one considers the primitive living conditions and the often filthy tasks performed, it is hardly surprising that cleanliness was not considered to be a priority.

In addition to their coarse linen clothing, the younger daughters and maidservants of a family would wear a *jupp* or short gown. This was close fined on the upper part of the body and was well suited for the performance of domestic or farm work. It was made from a locally woven, striped, woollen cloth called *drugget*.[36] Again the Culzean account book for 1783–1798 confirms that this was the style of dress worn in south Ayrshire too:

> May 27 1795. Betty Easton gave her £4 wages a short gown. No tea.

> Jan 1797. Peggy Webster a short gown & a muslin napkin as her last half years wages was small.[37]

The jerkin or coat worn by male servants and usually 'shortened in the skirts' was made from home spun wool which had been woven by the weaver and then taken to the waulk mill to be treated by the fuller. It was his task to beat and scour the fabric in order to both thicken it and remove from it unwanted dirt and grease. There was such a waulk mill in Kirkmichael, and in various kirk session minutes for Maybole and the surrounding villages, one comes across numerous references to both weavers and home spinning. The woven fabric produced was 'almost always blue.'[38]

Frequently, men left their shirt collar unbuttoned at the neck unless 'anything was passed above it, and round the neck of the wearer, it was often a shred of cloth carelessly folded and loosely tied'. On special occasions, or on the Sabbath or when going to market, a napkin might be worn.[39]

The napkin seems to have been a luxury item of dress as far as servants were concerned, and was sometimes given by a young man to a young female servant during courtship. Isobel McCulloch for example, a servant at Glengennet in the parish of Dailly, was courted by Robert Nimmo, her master's son, and given at various times, a napkin, the promise of a pair of shoes, three shillings and a pair of stockings.[40] In an important establishment like Culzean, napkins might be provided, the account book showing:

> April 1761. To Jenny & tiby Each a silk napkin

> April 1769. To Tibby Pebbles a Napkin 2/– [41]

The same account shows:

> 1759, Feb 23rd. Mutches for the Maids 5s.

> 1761, May. Each of the above a yd & $\frac{1}{4}$ Lace for a much (i.e. Jenny & Tiby)

According to the Rev. John Mitchell, when indoors, 'the females, particularly if elderly, always wore what was called a *mutch* or close cap made of coarse linen or flannel.'[42]

Many younger servants, both male and female went bareheaded, but older men might wear a woollen cap or 'when they went to Church or Market or Funeral put on a broad blue bonnet.'[43] Probably such bonnets would more often have been worn by tenant farmers rather than servants, although the 1792 *[Old] Statistical Account* for Symington comments 'the bonnet–makers of Kilmarnock, no longer find demand for their manufacture, from the servant men and labourers in this part of the country, but hats are worn by men and boys of all ranks.'[44]

Woollen hose, usually home–made, were worn, and both men and women were classed as stocking–makers. An example of this being that Ann Geddies, a servant in Craigoch, told Kirkoswald Kirk Session on 7th April 1765 that, 'about the beginning of the last shearing', John Brown, servant in Glenton, 'sat a Considerable time working his stocking, and left the kitchen a Considerable time before Robert Niven or she arose.' On 9 September 1764, the same kirk session was told by a witness that 'Hugh Alexander bad him not to be sore upon him, when he was Summoned as a witness by the Session', and he further added, that if he would do this, he would 'work him a pair of stockings.'[45]

The Rev. John Mitchell describes shoes as being plain and strong, fashioned from thick, rough, brown leather, often home tanned. They were usually fastened with leather thongs or latchets.[46] Robert Burns, in his letter from Ellisland to his brother William at Mossgiel on 5th May 1789, refers to such thongs.[47] The shoemaker Robert Anderson's account to which this letter refers includes shoes for two servants [see Illus. 13]. It was not unusual for a master to supply shoes for a servant. The *[Old] Statistical Account* for Dailly, for example, gives, 'the wages . . . of a female servant, 13s 4d with the perquisite of an apron and a pair of shoes.'[48] The Culzean accounts give:

      1755, June 2nd. To the Egg wife for shoes, 2s.

      1757, June 9th. To the Egg wife for shoes, 2s.

      July 8th. To shoes for a boy, 3s.

      Sept 9th. To Norrie for Shoes to Jenny, 3s and Davie.[49]

Some thirty years later the Kennedy of Kirkmichael papers record:

      1780. May: a pair Of shoes to Betty Gemmel, 2–6

      May. a pair of shoes to Rankin Kennedy, 5–0

      Aug. a pair of shoes to peggy ferguson, 1–8

      Dec. [similar], 1–8

      1781 Feb. [similar for] Betty Gemmel, 2–9

      March 2nd. [similar for] Betty Mcrother, 4–0 [50]

According to Rev. John Mitchell:

> shoes were not always worn. Boys, especially in summer, loved to go barefooted to school, housemaids did the same at home, and females, not even of the lower class, as well as thrifty house–wives, especially in earlier years, bearing their shoes and stockings, might be seen hieing away sturdily and alertly to the *neebor toon* on fair days or sacrament days, and at the close of the trip washing their feet and putting them on ere they went to the place of meeting.[51]

That account was written in 1780, and some two centuries later, at a meeting of Straiton Scottish Women's Rural Institute, I overheard two or three of the older members recall how they themselves used to walk barefoot from their homes on the farms to the outskirts of the village and then put on their clean shoes to attend the 'Rural' meeting.

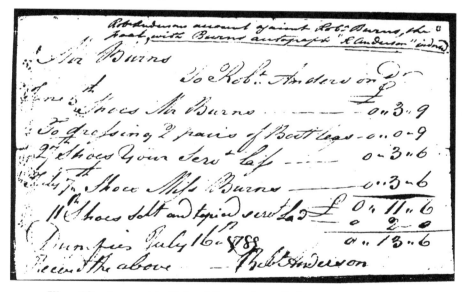

Illus. 13: Account to Robert Burns from Robert Anderson, Shoemaker, Dumfries, 1788. (Courtesy of Peter Westwood)

There are a few scattered references to underwear and night–clothes, like the Culzean account for January 1761 which records, '[a] pair of stays for Annie.'[52] As one might expect, the evidence given to the kirk sessions in cases of sexual scandal sometimes mentioned items of clothing as these examples show:

> Febr 25th 1761 . . . saw her comming from the Chamber one Night when the rest were in Bed, with her Cloaths all loose about her, and a cap in

her hand . . . The greater part of her Cloaths off having Nothing but her
Single Coat . . . she had on only her shirt and White Coat.[53]

Feb 4th 1789 . . . Having a Bedgown loose without a pin in it
hanging on one shoulder.[54]

The traditional eighteenth century outdoor wear for men was a plaid and
probably for many women servants too, although the Culzean accounts for
February 1763 show 'Cloke to Jenny.'[55] No price was given, so probably this was
an unwanted used garment. However, fashions were beginning to show signs of
change, as the Rev William Logan of Symington pointed out in his report to the
[Old] Statistical Account. Young women, including those of the lower ranks, no
longer wanted to wear the blue cloaks, red plaids, plain caps and scarlet mantles
which had been so desirable twenty years before. Instead, milk–maids adorned
themselves with silken coverings on their heads and shoulders and young men
rejected home–spun clothing in favour of 'English broadcloths, fashionable stripes,
and fine linen.'[56] Forty years before there were only three pocket watches in the
entire parish, but in 1792 all the youths sought to acquire one. It is hardly likely
that all the servants in the parish were able to keep pace with these changes in
fashion, but these were probably the aspirations of the younger members of the
servant class.

Clothing might be provided for servants for special occasions. In 1795,
Jane Gordon, a dairymaid at Culzean, was mentioned: 'when her fr Died gave her a
cheap gown about 7sh.'[57] On the other hand William Douglas had to purchase his
own clothes:

April 1794 William Douglas is to get £22 ster. a year when Lord L.
is Commissr rises to £27 as he is to get £5 more if he is made an Usher. He
furnished himself with all manner of Cloaths, as the other Ushers, and a suit
of Light Coloured Cloth Cloaths of Lord Levens Choosing.[58]

The funeral of an important personage was an occasion for outfitting the
servants with mourning clothes. No expense seems to have been spared for the
funeral of James Boswell's father, Lord Auchinleck, in August 1782. For the
coachmen and footmen, an Edinburgh cloth merchant provided 11½ yards grey
cloth, 14 yards shalloon (a light woollen stuff for coat linings), 3 cocked hats, 7½
yards crape, 5 pairs hose and 3 gloves. An Edinburgh tailor charged for making 3
suits of mourning. He also supplied 51 big and 6 doz. small buttons, silk and twist,
buckram binding and thread, 5 pockets for each frock and vest, pockets and
worsted garters, green linen sleeve linings and 7½ yards sage flannel. The list of
materials supplied by an Ayr merchant was extensive, comprising 6⅞ yards fine
black cloth, 6¾ yards shalloon, 5¾ yards plaiding, 4 yards stenting and pocketing,
1½ yards buckram, 7 ounces thread, 4 yards stay–tape, 3 dozen big and 4 dozen

small buttons, $1^3/_8$ yards fustian (coarse, twilled cotton fabric, including moleskin, velveteen, corduroy etc.), 1 pair knee garters, 22 yards crape, 21 drop silk and twist, $16¾$ yards broad black mankie (Calamanco – a satin–twilled woollen stuff; chequered or brocaded in the warp), 3 pairs of black out–sized stockings, $3½$ yards Italian hat crape, 4 yards black ribbon, 2 yards linen, $5¼$ yards muslin, 4 handkerchiefs, 2 pairs gloves, 2 hats, 16 yards black flannel, 2 women's gloves, 2 pairs black buckles and 12 yards tape. He also charged for making a suit of man's clothes.

The mourning clothes for the women servants seem to have been made at Auchinleck House, where there was an account for 'making servant–maids' caps, aprons and petticoats etc'. The servants in Lady Auchinleck's Edinburgh household had new outfits made from much more costly fabric than that thought necessary for the staff of a country estate.[59]

Illus. 14:   The staff of Kirkmichael House (undated).   (Ayrshire Archives, Kennedy of Kirkmichael Papers, ATD 64/11)

Because the appearance of certain servants could help to promote the status of the aristocracy, an act of the Scottish Parliament in 1672 permitted pages and lackeys of certain privileged persons excepted from an act forbidding the wearing of silks, laces and passments, which they 'may wear on their livery clothes.'[60]

Since the greater part of a servant's waking day was spent working, clothing would become worn out and discarded, so that one would not expect any items to have survived. Recently, however, livery items, found at Mount Stuart on Bute, were auctioned at Christie's in Glasgow. It is possible that these were identical to those worn at Dumfries House, Cumnock, since both establishments are and were owned by the same family. The find yielded

> eight mustard coloured footmen's felt jackets trimmed with red, blue and white, and bearing large silver buttons with the Bute coat of arms and rope twists on the shoulders. In the same lot are four navy blue cape coats and two pairs of black leather boots. Also . . . three footman's uniforms with brass buttoned black woollen tailcoats, matching waistcoats, blue velvet hose trimmed with gold brocade and two pairs of leather trousers.[61]

The male footmen who wore these clothes would also have had to powder their hair. The Bargany accounts for the period 1821–23 show that each of the named footmen were allowed a guinea per annum to pay for hair powder.[62]

Illus. 15: A domestic servant on a home visit to her family living in a cottage in the Muirkirk area. (Baird Institute, Cumnock)

Ayrshire servants do not appear to have had their portraits painted like those who lived at Erddig in Wales or *The Hen Wife of Castle Grant*. Genre paintings such as Sir David Wilkie's *The Cottar's Saturday Night* or *The Penny Wedding* give a general indication of the servant costume of his own time and his own locality. Photographs ought to provide a specific record of nineteenth century Ayrshire costume, but only two have been located and these are undated. One shows the staff of Kirkmichael House, probably taken sometime in the second half of the nineteenth century (Illus. 14). The other shows the occupants of a cottage in the Muirkirk area and included a domestic servant on a visit home to her family (Illus. 15).

In 1825 Samuel and Sarah Adams, an English couple, with first–hand experience of being in domestic service themselves, published *The Complete Servant*, which claimed to give advice to servants in general, but in all probability it provided their employers with advice.[63] In respect of clothing, the young lady's maid might expect to receive 'her mistress' left off clothes.' The butler and the valet might also expect the perquisites of their master's cast off clothes. The footman was expected to provide his own linen stockings, shoes and washing, but if he was required to wear silk, then it had to be provided by the family employing him. When he left his position, he was required to leave behind any livery items that he had received in the previous six months. His newest livery was to be kept for wear on Sundays and special occasions. For work, such as cleaning, he usually wore 'a pair of overalls, a waistcoat and fustian jacket, and a leather apron, with a white one to put on occasionally, when called from these duties.' He could expect to receive, 'two livery and two undress suits per annum.' The lady's footman could expect, 'two liveries and a working dress' and the under footman 'liveries.'

The head coachman must have been a fine figure to behold, with 'his flaxen curls or wig, his low cocked hat, his plush breeches, and his benjamin surcoat, his clothes also being well brushed and the lace and buttons in a high state of polish.' The under, second, or lady's coachman might expect to be supplied with two suits of livery, a box coat occasionally, hat and boots, also one or two stable dresses. These liveries were 'not always quite so costly' as those of their senior. For the groom there should be 'two livery suits and two stable dresses a year', with nearly the same for the postillion, 'only that he had a cap, and generally a jacket instead of a frock coat.' In smaller families, the groom and valet or footman would have had to make do with 'cast off clothes.' The stable boy's clothing was 'as may be agreed' and the helper in the stables was to wear 'the same as the grooms.'[64]

One cannot be sure that these standards of dress were reached in the larger establishments in Ayrshire, but it is more than likely that they were at Culzean where livery buttons were frequently purchased, at Dumfries House, at Auchincruive with its fine stables and at Bargany, where John Hamilton had a splendid coach built. When Debbie Jackson interviewed people who had worked at Culzean during the time of the third Marquis (1870–1938), she learned that the butler wore a livery consisting of a blue double breasted jacket with polished brass buttons and blue trousers, and the footman's light blue uniform had gold stripes along the arms and along the outside length of each leg, and each of his buttons bore the Kennedy coat of arms. The coachman had a blue uniform with black leather boots trimmed with brown leather, and his tall hat sported a big rosette on the side of it. The grooms, gardeners and laundry maids wore their own clothes, the latter being told only to wear dark garments. The housemaids wore black dresses with white aprons and caps.[65] Mrs Hume, who had been in service at Bargany and Lochinch, as well as the Buccleuch establishments, recalled that the male servants wore their uniforms to attend church, and the women wore black frocks with toques or bonnets. She added, 'You didn't get going in coloured clothes and you sat up in the gallery.'[66] She also recalled that the waiters never wore gloves where she was, but they had linen slips – washed and ironed by the laundry maids – 'clean ones every day they had – a kind of ritual.' And 'at Christmas, Lady Marjorie gave you the making of a blouse when she was alive.'

Writing in 1952, Marjorie Plant, quoting from both the *[Old] Statistical Account* and from *Glasgow, Past and Present*, said 'the road from Portpatrick to Dumfries swarmed with Irish beggars. One class of them called troggers, brought Irish linen which they were glad to barter for old woollen clothes. But elsewhere old clothes were hardly ever sold. They were either given away in charity or used by servants for dusters or floor cloths.'[67]

Elizabeth C. Sanderson, writing about Edinburgh, provided considerable detail regarding the pawning of clothes. She found that the poor pawned their clothes from necessity, and the middle classes because there was a shortage of coins in the eighteenth century.[68] Kirk session records show the presence of troggers in south Ayrshire, so old clothes may well have been traded in the locality as in Galloway. The actual pawning of clothes may have happened on a small scale in private deals, although no evidence has been found to show this.

The clothing of those who had the misfortune to end up in the poor house became the property of either the Board of the Poorhouse, or of the local Inspector of the Poor, upon the death of the inmate. The minute book of Maybole Combination Poorhouse (1865–1876) reveals something of the extent and state of the clothing. On 27th December 1866, the Governor of the Poorhouse brought to the board meeting the clothing of the paupers who had died during the year. The coat, vest and trousers that had been worn by Thomas Gait, Peter Purcell and Thomas Moodie were given to the Inspector of the Poor for Maybole as was a silver watch which, surprisingly, had been in the possession of Thomas Moodie.[69] Margaret Findlay's clothing being but a bundle of rags was given to the Matron for washing cloths, and the clothing of Agnes Carruthers and Janet Bruce was so old that it was destroyed, except for a plaid which had belonged to Carruthers, and which by sanction of the Inspector of the Poor for Maybole was given to Ann McKinlay for her children.

As the nineteenth century progressed, domestic servants were required to wear uniforms, not only in the houses of the aristocracy and the gentry, but also in the houses of many employers of lesser status. To cater for these requirements, shops in Ayr began to stock ready–made clothing for servants, one such being located in the Sandgate, and which advertised 'A large assortment of Servants' Aprons, Caps, and Wrappers Always in Stock.'[70] Records of local prices for these items do not seem to have survived, but those listed in the surviving catalogues of The Army and Navy Co–operative Society, which may have supplied the households of masters with an armed service background, give some indication of prevailing prices.

Since clothing can be used to make a statement about the wearer, it was usually possible to identify a servant by the clothing being worn, although on the smaller farms the masters and servants may have worn similar attire.

MISSES A. & A BOYD,

DRESSMAKERS AND DRAPERS,

71 SANDGATE, AYR.

Ladies' and Children's Underclothing,

Hosiery, Blouses, Belts, Ribbons, Gloves, Laces,

and Fancy Goods.

ooOOOoo

A LARGE ASSORTMENT OF

Servants' Aprons, Caps, and Wrappers

ALWAYS ON STOCK.

Illus. 16: Advertisement promoting the sale of clothes for servants which appeared in the *Ayr Post Office General and Trades Directory for Ayr, Newton and Wallacetown* (1912–1913). (Carnegie Library, Ayr)

SERVANTS' COATS.

Coachmen's Capes, with sleeves.

All seams sewn and taped.

	Length. Chest.	Length. Chest.	Length. Chest.	Length. Chest.	Length. Chest.
Stock sizes—	40 by 42 in. ...	42 by 44 in. ...	44 by 46 in. ...	46 by 48 in. ...	48 by 50 in.
To fit—	5 ft. 4 in. ...	5 ft. 6 in. ...	5 ft. 8 in. ...	5 ft. 10 in. ...	6 ft. 0 in.
Best quality black cashmere					40/3
2nd ,, ,, ,,					31/3
Best ,, white glazed proof					37/6
2nd ,, ,, ,, ,,					32/9
3rd ,, ,, ,, ,,					28/3

Footmen's or Groom's Coats.

All seams sewn and taped.

Stock sizes—	48 by 40 in. ...	50 by 42 in. ...	52 by 44 in. ...	54 by 44 in. ...	56 by 48 in.
To fit—	5 ft. 4 in. ...	5 ft. 6 in. ...	5 ft. 8 in. ...	5 ft. 10 in. ...	6 ft. 0 in.
Best quality black cashmere					38/6
2nd ,, ,,					29/9
Best ,, white glazed proof					37/3
2nd ,, ,, ,, ,,					32/6
3rd ,, ,, ,, ,,					26/6

All Servants' Coats are fitted with Velvet Collars.

The above Glazed Coats can be procured to order in Black Proof.

Self measurement form on application.   Special measures extra.

Illus. 17: Extract from the Army & Navy Stores Catalogue, March, 1908. (University of Glasgow Archives, HF6/9/2)

[1] A.P.S. 1617, c8, §14, IV 537; 1661, c338, VII 308

[2] Aiton, William, *General View of Agriculture in the County of Ayr*, [Glasgow, 1811], p. 517.

[3] Fullarton, Col. William *General View of the County of Ayr*, [Edinburgh, 1793], p. 72.

[4] Jackson, Debbie, "History of the Kennedys", unpublished ms., pp. 63–65.

[5] N.A.S., Ailsa Muniments, GD 25/9/19.

[6] Poor Law Inquiry (Scotland), Appendix IV, 1844.

[7] *Ayr Advertiser*, 6th March 1879.

[8] Report of the Royal Commission on Labour, Vol III Scotland, Part I, B II.

[9] *ibid.*

[10] *ibid.*

[11] Aiton, William, *General View of the Agriculture in the County of Ayr*, [Glasgow, 1811], p.117–118.

[12] *Acts Gen. Ass., The Assembly's Pastoral Address on the Increase of Immorality in the Rural Districts*, [Edinburgh, 1861], p.79.

[13] Aiton, William *Ayrshire General view of Agriculture in the County of Ayr*, [Glasgow, 1811], p.125.

[14] Report by J.H. Tremenheere, 1867.

[15] *ibid.*

[16] *Royal Commission on Labour, The Agricultural Labourer* Vol. III, *Scotland Part 1 Parliamentary Papers*; 1893, p.56, para 44.

[17] A.A., Hamilton of Rozelle and Carcluie Papers, SAC/DC 17/1174 Bundle 115.

[18] *ibid*, Bundle 129.

[19] Stamp, Gavin, *Robert Weir Schulz–Architect and his work for the Marquesses of Bute. An Essay*, [London, 1981].

[20] Mure, Elizabeth, as quoted in *Scottish Diaries and Memoirs 1746–1843*, J.G. Fyfe, ed., [Stirling, 1942], p.64.

[21] Varley, Charles, *The Modem Farmers Guide*, [Edinburgh, 1768], as quoted in Clarke, Desmond, *The Unfortunate Husbandman*, [London, 1964], p.85–86.

[22] Graham, Henry Grey, *The Social Life of Edinburgh in the Eighteenth Century*, [London 1937], p.179.

[23] N.A.S., Ailsa Muniments, GD25/9/19.

[24] Galt, John *Annals of the Parish*, [London 1895], p.12.

[25] Aiton, William, *General View of Agriculture in the County of Ayr*, [Glasgow. 1811], p.653–6.

[26] Strawhorn, John, *The History of Ayr, Royal Burgh and County Town* ,[Edinburgh, 1989], p.152.

[27] A.A., Ayrshire Sound Archive, ASA 077, *Life in Domestic Service 1*.

[28] A.A., Ayrshire Sound Archive, ASA 078, *Life in Domestic Service 2*.

[29] Ayr Advertiser, 23rd September 1875.

[30] A.P.S. 1621, C25 § § 6, 7, IV 626.

[31] N.A.S., Ailsa Muniments, GD 25/9/19.

[32] Smout, T.C., *A History of the Scottish People 1560–1830* [London, 1971], p.142.

[33] Mitchell, Rev. John, "Memories of Ayrshire about 1780", in *Miscellany of the Scottish History Society, 6*, [Edinburgh, 1939], p.262–266.

[34] A.A., Kirkoswald Kirk Session Minutes, CH2/562/2, 1st December 1778.

[35] Mitchell, Rev. John, "Memories of Ayrshire about 1780", in *Miscellany of the Scottish History Society, 6*, [Edinburgh, 1939], pp. 262–266.

[36] *ibid.*

[37] N.A.S., Ailsa Muniments, GD 25/9/19.

[38] Mitchell, Rev. John, "Memories of Ayrshire about 1780", in *Miscellany of the Scottish History Society, 6*, [Edinburgh, 1939], pp 262–266.

[39] *ibid.*

[40] A.A., Dailly Kirk Session Minutes, CH2/392/3, 11th December 1774.

[41] N.A.S., Ailsa Muniments, GD 25/9/19.

[42] Mitchell, Rev. John, "Memories of Ayrshire about 1780", in *Miscellany of the Scottish History Society, 6*, [Edinburgh, 1939], pp.262–266.

[43] *ibid.*

[44] *[Old] Statistical Account* Vol. V p.403–404.

[45] A.A., Kirkoswald Kirk Session Minutes, CH2/562/2.

[46] Mitchell, Rev. John, "Memories of Ayrshire about 1780", in *Miscellany of the Scottish History Society, 6*, [Edinburgh, 1939], pp.262–266.

[47] Burns, Robert, Letter to William Burns 5th May, 1789, printed in *The Complete Letters of Robert Burns*, James A MacKay, ed., [Alloway, 1990], p 516.

[48] *[Old] Statistical Account* Vol. V, p. 137.

[49] N.A.S., Ailsa Muniments, GD 25/9/19.

[50] A.A., Kennedy of Kirkmichael Papers, ATD 42/3/148.

[51] Mitchell, Rev John, "Memories of Ayrshire about 1780", in *Miscellany of the Scottish History Society 6*, [Edinburgh, 1939], pp 262–266.

[52] N.A.S., Ailsa Muniments, GD 25/9/19.

[53] A.A., Kirkmichael Kirk Session Minutes, CH2/1333/1.

[54] A.A., Dailly Kirk Session Minutes, CH2/392/3.

[55] N.A.S., Ailsa Muniments, GD 25/9/19.

[56] *[Old] Statistical Account* Vol V, p.403–404.

[57] N.A.S., Ailsa Muniments, GD 25/9/19.

[58] *ibid.*

[59] Reed, Joseph W. & Pottle, Frederick, eds., *Boswell, Laird of Auchinleck*, [Edinburgh. 1993], pp.483–487.

[60] A.P.S. 1672, c.21, V11 72a.

[61] *The Herald*, 23rd March 1996.

[62] N.A.S., Bargany Papers, GD 109/2931.

[63] Adams, Samuel & Sarah, *The Complete Servant*, 1825. Horn, Pamela, *Introduction to the Complete Servant*, [Lewes. East Sussex, 1989].

[64] *ibid.*

[65] Jackson, Debbie, "History of the Kennedys", unpublished ms.

[66] A.A., Ayrshire Sound Archive, ASA 071, 1984, *Life in Domestic Service*.

[67] Plant, Marjorie, *The Domestic Life of Scotland*, [Edinburgh, 1952], p.201.

[68] Sanderson, Elizabeth C., *Women and Work in Eighteenth–Century Edinburgh*, [London, 1996], p 150.

[69] A.A., Maybole Combination Poorhouse Board minute book 1865–1876, CO3/50/1/4/1.

[70] *Ayr Post Office General and Trades Directory for Ayr. Newton, and Wallacetown*, 1912–1913.

Chapter 4: Population Changes

Migration to another place of service

The Hearth Tax records for Carrick provide evidence of the existence of many dwellings whose locations do not appear on any of the local maps or whose names are unfamiliar to a number of people well acquainted with the area.[1] It would appear that many people were displaced when sheep farming was introduced, or when several small farms were combined to form a larger unit. According to Strawhorn,[2] the creation in the seventeenth century of new parishes like New Cumnock, Barr, Sorn and Stair, possibly indicated a movement of surplus population into the less attractive parts of the country in search of marginal land.

The extent of the population decrease in the parish of Barr during the previous 30 years was described in the *Old Statistical Account:* 'in place of a family with cottages and servants upon almost every farm, there are some farms in which is not one inhabitant, and many where a shepherd man servant and his family alone occupy there the farm.'[3] The Colmonell report detailed the practice of inclosures that, coupled with the increase in rents, 'occasioned the dismission of herds and cottages', and the consequent depletion of the local population.[4] The Rev. James Mochrie summed up this eighteenth century form of 'downsizing' thus:

> About twenty years ago there was hardly a tenant who had not one or more of these cottages on his farm, whereas now there are very few of them in the whole parish–The cottages were the nurseries of the servants, but their inhabitants have now been removed to towns, and have bred up their children to other employments, farm servants have become exceedingly scarce throughout the whole country.[5]

Girvan, the nearest town to Barr and Colmonell, reported an estimated population increase from 100 to 1000 within 40 to 50 years.[6] This was attributed to the herring glut, the enclosures with the consequential rural depopulation and the practice of smuggling. Herring would have provided cheap, nutritious food for the dispossessed cottagers and servants who migrated to the town and villages. Since these were able–bodied poor, they and their families would not qualify for poor relief. Necessity may have forced many into the smuggling trade if they lacked the skills to pursue a trade in the town and were unable to find a place in service in what must have been a highly competitive market at that time. The majority of these unfortunate people would have died before the first census was taken. Those who entered the smuggling trade were sometimes vulnerable to being abducted and pressed into service in the navy. An anonymous nineteenth century writer about eighteenth century Carrick noted that a press gang frequently surrounded the Ship Inn at Girvan and an unnamed inn in Ballantrae. He added:

We have it recorded that when H.M. Ship Berwick anchored in Lochryan in 1792 there were procured 80 volunteers from Girvan, Ballantrae and Stranraer for service against the King's enemies . . . the said volunteers were carried on board bound hand and foot.[7]

Apart from these clearances, migration to another place of service would appear to have been the main cause of migration in south Ayrshire. Among the miscellaneous notes provided by James Gillespie is a reference to the Presbytery of Ayr records commenting upon the frequent movement of farm servants, the extent of which was 'best understood at Whitsunday when those leaving for another parish, come to 'lift their lines.' On an average a fifth of the members on a Communion Roll do this (every year), so that, practically, the population is changed once in five years.'[8]

The poor law records reveal in considerable detail the itinerant life that some servants had led before becoming destitute. Jane Dixon, a 29 year old, pregnant domestic servant, and her two children aged 12 and 6 were given temporary relief on 8th May 1863 in Maybole Combination Poorhouse, having been deserted by her husband, a 44 year old drainer and labourer. They had both been born in Ireland, where they lived with their daughter, until crossing to Stranraer, where they lived three or four years at Greenvale. Then they spent ten months at Redburn, Ballantrae, two or three months at Girvan, where their son was born, before returning to Redburn for six months. Next they stayed fully three years in Colmonell, then a year in Girvan, four months at Kirkland, and finally eleven months in Maybole. The parochial Board agreed to return the family to Ireland.[9]

On 28th October 1863 Elizabeth Chancellor, a 23 year old farm servant, gave birth to a wholly disabled illegitimate child named John. The putative father of the child was Francis Robertson, a farm servant belonging to Kirkoswald parish, who was supposed to have gone to America. Elizabeth, who had been born in Ireland, lived in Maybole with her Irish father, but he had turned her out of his house two weeks before her application for poor relief, the day after she gave birth to the child. Since leaving Ireland, she had spent six months at Maidens Shore, six months at Dabrioch, four months with her father at Pat's Corner, Maybole, eight months at Mr. Millan's Tileworks at Dalrymple, six months at Brae by Girvan, a month with her father at Pat's Corner, Maybole, two months at Kirkbrae, Girvan, three months at Barcullie by Crosshill, Kirkmichael, two years at Shalloch, Girvan, two months at Fullerton in Irvine, two months with her father at Pat's Corner, and finally two weeks at Smithy Brae, Maybole, where the child was born and she was confined to bed. The Board gave her temporary relief, and then returned her to Ireland.[10]

Obviously these sad cases would be extreme, but it does indicate how insecure a servant's life could be. They also illustrate some of the difficulties Irish migrants could experience in seeking settlement in Scotland, or even trying to keep a family together when only temporary situations might be available and there might not be work for both parents in the same locality, and the wage of one parent being insufficient to support the family. Some would find the strain too much, as may have been the case with the above–mentioned Dixon family.

Many male Irish migrants came by the short sea crossing to Portpatrick and passed through south Ayrshire seeking employment in the coalfields, heavy metal industries, digging canals or building railways. Others came to dig ditches to drain the fields or labour in the potato fields. These were usually temporary migrants who returned to Ireland each year when their contracts were concluded. This use of temporary contract labour helped to reduce the number of servants employed on the farms. Irish women too worked in the potato fields. In 1869, the chief constable of Ayrshire estimated that there were some 10,000 vagrants in the country and that about three–fifths of them were Irish, but as James Handley has observed, most of these were 'migratory labourers moving about the country to help in the grain and potato harvests.'[11] One result of this migration into the area was to offset the reduction of the population caused by both emigration and mortality and to raise the local fertility rates because typically it was the young of both sexes who tended to migrate, and when their numbers were brought further into balance, population tended to increase.[12]

The latter part of the eighteenth century saw the transition from home based industry to larger, capital backed enterprises. This applied particularly in the textile industry where much of the traditional spinning and weaving of wool which could be combined with domestic duties, was, after a brief flirtation with linen, overtaken by cotton, which created a demand for labour.

In particular, this was the case in the Catrine Mill, founded in 1787, employing 200 persons in 1790, 301 by 1796,[13] and by 1837, the cotton and bleaching works employed 913 workers (315 males and 598 females).[14] These workers had migrated from 'different parts of the Kingdom.'[15] This local abundance of work forced up wages as farmers and others competed with the Catrine works for labour.[16] Early in the nineteenth century a demand was created for Ayrshire Embroidery, a type of whitework. Agents in Ayr and Glasgow employed many hundreds of home based women *flowerers*. The *New Statistical Account* report for Tarbolton noted that 'girls of a more tender age (than 10 or 11) earn their substance at needlework', which would indicate that they would be less likely to be available for domestic and agriculture service.[17] Here where 'a large proportion of the females were engaged in sewing, the work was of a high standard, and the payment received the main source of income for many families.'[18] The *[Old] Statistical Account* report for Ochiltree commented that 'considerable number of young females in the village and in some parts of the country are employed in sewing muslin.'[19] It deplored the health risks they faced and their lack of training in domestic skills and management. Some 300 females in Ayr were engaged in this work,[20] including 50–60 who resided in Newton–upon–Ayr.[21] In Sorn, in 1837, quite apart from the Catrine workers, there were three sewing mistresses, 100 hand sewers, five white seam sewers and six cloth merchants.[22] 'A number of women, older and younger', were employed in sewing in Auchinleck.[23]

Wages for sewing could range from 4d–2s per day, depending upon skill and market conditions. Despite the eye–strain involved, many women would have preferred sewing to service, because it would suit their domestic and child care responsibilities, and because it could be sociable, the work being done outside in good weather, or by a number of women sharing a 'puir man' candlestick in the evening.[24] The outbreak of the American Civil War resulted in the collapse of the cotton industry, and a time of great hardship for the workers, some of whom may well have been willing to seek employment in service.

The enclosures and farm amalgamations in many of the parishes, required servants to seek work elsewhere. Although it cannot compare with the north of the county, some heavy industry did offer employment to men, notably in Muirkirk and Dalmellington.

The coming of the railway in the 1840s helped to turn the coastal towns into seaside resorts and create domestic employment in servicing the visitors. In Monkton and Prestwick for example, according to the 1841 Census, there were 52 servants,[25] but by 1861, this number had increased to 115,[26] and by 1891, there were 42 domestic servants, 68 general servants, 51 housekeepers, 22 cooks, 10 coachmen, 4 butlers, 13 housemaids, 5 kitchenmaids, 7 nurses and nursemaids, 5 tablemaids and 3 footmen.[27] Allowing for those who were family members of the household there does seem to have been a remarkable growth in the servant population in what was a typical seaside resort.

Emigration

Apart from the names of those criminals who were sentenced to transportation, there is a distinct lack of information about most of those who emigrated in the eighteenth century from Ayrshire. It seems likely that some would serve under Col. Hugh Montgomery (later 12th Earl of Eglinton) in the American War of Independence, and settled in North America at the end of hostilities, possibly with a land grant. A number of kirk session records include cases of unmarried women with child in which the reputed father had 'gone to America', but, apart from his name, no further details were given.

Prior to the American War of Independence, emigration was likely to have been to the West Indies or the American colonies. Robert Burns and it is presumed Margaret Campbell (*Highland Mary*) had planned a new life in Jamaica[28] and local landowners like Robert Hamilton of Bourtreehill and Rozelle had plantations there, so people would be aware of these overseas colonies.

A letter from Gabriel Cathcart of North Carolina offered work to a man from Ballantrae of humble origin, who had been in 'country service most of his life.' His duty would be to oversee a few blacks, in return for his bed and board and £7 sterling a year, with his passage money being 'deducted from his first year's pay.'[29] In the American colonies a class system existed, with indentured servants only a marginal level above the black slaves; indeed in the seventeenth century these indentured servants had been more important than the blacks as a labour force.[30] There was a legal code in each colony to govern indentured servants. They were supposed to be fed, clothed, and well treated, but often conditions were so bad that they ran away from their masters. 'At the end of their indenture, many were given land and were able to enter the ranks of the middle class.' The majority of the Presbyterian Scotch–Irish people largely settled in Virginia and the Carolinas, where they became something of a threat to the political power of the upper class. Unless they had sufficient savings or could borrow the money, which was most unlikely, servants emigrating from this country would have to be indentured, a facility available to both men and women.

After 1815, British public opinion regarded the Empire as a solution to the problems created by its surplus population. There was concern that there would be too great a charge upon public funds if the number of paupers was permitted to increase. Efforts were made to encourage emigration.

A government advertisement placed in the *Air Advertiser* on 2nd March 1815, offered land grants of 100 acres in either Upper or Lower Canada to families willing to become settlers there. A deposit of £16 sterling was required for men and two guineas for their wives, the money being returnable two years after settlement there. Children under 16 years were to be conveyed free of expense, and all male children were to be given a similar land grant when they reached 21 years of age. Departure from an allocated Clyde port to the port of Quebec was to be that April. The government would pay the cost of the passage and provisions for the journey, and on arrival the settlers could obtain axes and other tools at less than half price, and be supplied with rations from the public store for the first 6–8 months in order to allow them time to establish themselves and to clear and cultivate a portion of their land. The settlers had to supply character testimonials, but since these were normally required when people moved from one parish to another, this would not be considered unusual. Where a number of families originating from the same locality decided to settle in the same neighbourhood, care would be taken to allot them, 'lands as nearly as possible contiguous with each other'.[31] Perhaps this accounts for a place called Monkton in Ontario (43° 35' N, 81° 06' W).

The people who would avail themselves of this government offer would be the small tenant farmers who could no longer afford to pay rent or who wished to own their own land, and skilled farm servants who could not secure a farm tenancy or a situation for a married farm servant. Their wives may well have spent time as servants, and their children, instead of entering the servant class here, would hope to become farmers or their wives in the New World. Few emigrants can have realised just how hard their life was to be or the problems they were to encounter with unscrupulous land agents. In general, emigrants were given passage on vessels which had carried timber from North America. The *Air Advertiser* of 9th March 1815 reported the arrival at Troon on 18th February of 'Lancaster, Anderson, from the bay of Chaleur, North America, with a cargo of timber, to Hew MacKissock and Co.'[32]

When T. F. Kennedy was examined by the Select Committee of Emigration in 1827, and was asked if his distressed cotton weavers had knowledge of the difficulties likely to be encountered in America, he replied that, 'the county of Ayr is a part of the country from which persons have often proceeded to America.'[33] After the American War of Independence, 1775–83, and the British–American War of 1812–14, encouragement was given to people to settle in Canada and to act as a bulwark against further American expansion. It seems highly likely that some of the displaced servants from Ayrshire might have found their way there. They would no doubt have made good settlers, for as Professor E. J. Cowan has pointed out, 'agriculturists have to be able to turn their hands to a variety of diverse tasks simply because there is no–one else to do them',[34] and this would certainly be the case in the totally undeveloped land they had to transform. Mary Storie, who lived in Galloway and Ayrshire before she emigrated to Canada in 1828, wrote to her father, Osborn Macqueen, and referring to her younger sister suggested 'if Janet is still continuing in the servant way, I think this is the country for her; as a servant here is equal to her mistress and receives from 4 to 5 dollars per month.'[35] Janet married, lived and died in Scotland, but others may have decided to better their circumstances in the New World. The *New Statistical Account* report for Dailly noted 'emigration has not much prevailed in this neighbourhood, but is upon the increase',[36] and that for Barr reported 'the supernumeraries, beyond the farms and labour, slip off, as they rise up, to towns or other parts of the country, and not a few go abroad.'[37]

In the mid nineteenth century, the United Provinces of Canada tried to promote immigration with a policy which included a payment to a Mrs. C. P. Trail for 600 copies of a reputedly entertaining book entitled, *The Female Emigrant's Guide and Companion.* Obviously, where the initial phase of settlement was complete, the need arose for single women to serve in the avenues open to women at that time, and to help populate the country.

An advertisement in the *Ayr Advertiser* of 26th September 1861 offered free emigration to Tasmania for 100 experienced ploughmen, 20 dairymaids, 20 laundrymaids, 30 housemaids, 20 nurserymaids, 20 female cooks, and 30 married farm servants preferably without children.   Interviews were conducted in Kilmarnock, Ayr, Maybole and Girvan, and those applicants selected were to sail from Glasgow three months later.[38] It also advertised half price fares to Otago, New Zealand, for suitable females proceeding to the Colony'.[39]   After the Disruption of the Established Church of Scotland in 1843, the Rev. Thomas Burns of Monkton and Prestwick, a nephew of the poet, emigrated to Otago with a large proportion of his congregation, and it seems likely that some families would have taken their servants with them. When gold–fields were discovered in the vicinity in 1861, immigrants flocked there to seek their fortune, and no doubt those who succeeded required servants to cook and clean for them.[40]

When disaster befell the textile industry, there was a surge of emigration and the families who left the country may have included some in service. By 1881, the Cape Mounted Riflemen were advertising for single youths from 20–26 years of age who were farm lads, grooms, farriers and others accustomed to horses, cattle and agriculture pursuits.[41]

Professor Devine has described emigration as 'but an extension on migration within Scotland',[42] and it does seem to be the case that many of the servant class in particular led a semi–nomadic existence both within the U.K. and overseas. As more and more people try to trace their family histories on both sides of the Atlantic and Australia, it may be possible to construct a clearer picture of the emigration of servants in the eighteenth and nineteenth centuries.

[1] Urquhart, Robert H. J. and Close, Rob, ed., *The Hearth Tax for Ayrshire 1691,* [Ayr 1998].

[2] Strawhorn, John, "Ayrshire's Changing Population" in *Ayrshire Collections*, Vol.8, Second Series, 1967–9, pp. 12–13.

[3] *[Old] Statistical Account* Vol. VI, p. 57.

[4] *[Old] Statistical Account* Vol. VI, p. 89.

[5] *ibid.*

[6] *[Old] Statistical Account* Vol. VI, p. 232/233.

[7] [Anon.], *Carrick in the Eighteenth Century,* undated manuscript. Copy in Carnegie Library, Ayr: 941.421.

[8] Gillespie, James, *Dundonald,* Vol. II, [Glasgow, 1939], p. 574.

[9] A.A., Maybole Parochial Board, Register of applications for parochial relief, 1855–65, CO3/50/1/3/7.

[10] *ibid.*

[11] Handley, James E. *The Irish in Scotland,* [Glasgow, 1947], p. 332.

[12] Flinn, Michael, et al., *Scottish Population History,* [Cambridge, 1977], p. 40.

[13] *[Old] Statistical Account* Vol. VI, p. 562.

[14] *New Statistical Account* Vol. V, p. 141.

[15] *[Old] Statistical Account* Vol. VI, p. 566.

[16] *ibid*, p. 533–534.

[17] *New Statistical Account* Vol. V, p. 763.

[18] *New Statistical Account* Vol. V, p. 759–760.

[19] *ibid*, p. 113.

[20] *ibid*, p. 54–55.

[21] *ibid*, p. 99.

[22] *ibid*, p. 137.

[23] *ibid*, p. 329.

[24] Bryson, Agnes F., *Ayrshire needlework*, [London, 1989], p.20.

[25] 1841 Census for Monkton & Prestwick.

[26] 1861 Census for Monkton & Prestwick.

[27] 1891 Census for Monkton & Prestwick.

[28] Sprott, Gavin, *Pride and Passion*, [Edinburgh, 1996], p.154.

[29] Brock, William R., *Scotus Americanus*, [Edinburgh, 1982], p.30.

[30] Craven, A. & Johnston, W., *The United States Experiment in Democracy,* [Chicago, 1957], p.62.

[31] *Air Advertiser*, 2nd March 1815.

[32] *ibid*, 9th March 1815.

[33] B.P.P. Report from the select Committee on Emigration 1827, para. 226. Emigration from the United Kingdom Vol.2, [Shannon, 1968].

[34] Cowan E.J., "Internal Migration in Nineteenth Century Scotland", in *Families* vol. 21, no. 4 (1982).

[35] Lyle, E.B. (ed) *Andrew Crawfurd's Collection of Ballads and Songs* Vol.2, [Edinburgh, 1996], p. xvi–xvii.

[36] *New Statistical Account* Vol. V. p.385.

[37] *New Statistical Account* Vol. V. p.410.

[38] *Ayr Advertiser*, 26th September 1861.

[39] *ibid*, 7th November 1861.

[40] *ibid*, 6th February 1862.

[41] *ibid*, 21st April 1881.

[42] Devine, T.M., ed., *Scottish Emigration and Scottish Society,* [Edinburgh, 1992], p.8.

Chapter 5: The Concerns of Everyday Life

Health Care, Retirement and Death

From the evidence which I have been able to examine, it appears that if they survived the hazards of childhood to become members of the servant class, most people could expect to die from old age or one of the diseases to which older people become vulnerable.   Plenty of fresh air, exercise and monotonous yet nutritious food would have done much to promote good health.

In the hill country of Carrick, there were a number of mineral springs said to have medicinal properties. These are mentioned in the *[Old] Statistical Account* reports of Ballantrae,[1] New Cumnock,[2] Old Cumnock,[3] Muirkirk,[4] and in the *New Statistical Account* report for Maybole.[5] In the *New Statistical Account* report for Dalrymple,[6] the minister mentioned the mineral spring near Skeldon which in 1798 had been used by the late Captain Campbell of Carbieston, who 'frequently made his servants drink it.'

Traditionally the mistress or housekeeper was expected to have knowledge of local plants with healing properties and to be able to concoct medicines for use in treating sick members of the household. Such knowledge and skills would be passed down to the daughters and maids who in their turn would have to assume responsibility for the care of ailments and sickness as they arose. Some advice could be sought from the minister, laird or schoolmaster, but in general it was the women who treated the sick; although in October 1766, a Mr. Bannerman was recorded as having a shop in Maybole where a drug could be purchased, so possibly this was an apothecary's shop.[7] On that occasion, the purchaser bought a brownish powder to give to a pregnant girl, who was to take it followed by a bitter apple in order to induce an abortion.

In September 1809, a Doctor David Robertson was recorded as having a shop in Girvan where people could 'buy something',[8] implying drugs and potions. In the time of Burns, schoolmasters were so poorly paid that many tried to supplement their income, as was the case with John Wilson, better remembered as the Dr. Hornbook who neglected his teaching for his shop in Tarbolton, where he dispensed medicines with sometimes unfortunate consequences.

Burns told the tale in his poem "Death and Doctor Hornbook", from which come the following lines:

> ... Hornbook's skill
> Has clad a score I' their last claith
> By drap and pill.
>
> . . .
>
> A bonnie lass, ye kenn'd her name
> Some ill–brewn drink had hov'd her wame'
> She trusts hersel', to hide her shame
> In Hornbook's care;
> Horn sent her off to her lang hame,
> To hide it there.

Several of the reports in the *New Statistical Account* list a number of the plants growing in their respective parishes and, by checking these against *The Scots Herbal,*[9] it is possible to gain some idea of the range of remedies available in these localities. Although one cannot be sure which were used in practice, there were more than fifty different plants with medicinal properties growing in south Ayrshire. Sphagnum moss, which contains penicillin, was to be found in Muirkirk,[10] and probably in the mosses of other parishes before they were drained. This moss could be used to dress wounds and reduce the chances of infection. It could be used like toilet paper, sanitary towels or as disposable nappies.[11] The elder (*Sambucus*) is listed in the Coylton[12] and Dundonald[13] reports in the *New Statistical Account,* but it must have grown in other parishes for traditionally, like the rowan *(Sorbus)*, it was planted to protect the occupants from witches and other malevolent spirits.

Possibly this magical connection accounts for the many and varied medical uses the elder was thought to have.[14] The whole plant could be used as a purgative, an emetic or a diuretic. Its bark and root could be used in the treatment of 'dropsy, epilepsy, asthma, and croup.' An ointment could be prepared from its leaves and applied to 'bruises, sprains, chilblains, wounds, dropsy, inflamed eyes, blocked nose, and to treat nervous headaches.' The flowers were used in the treatment of 'wounds, burns, chilblains and other skin problems, scarlet fever, measles and other diseases that cause rashes and spots, pleurisy, constipation, colds, sore throats, flu, inflamed eyes, pain, headaches, piles.' The berries were used as 'remedies for rheumatism, syphilis, constipation, colic, diarrhoea, epilepsy, and piles.' Elderberry wine could be drunk for 'catarrh, flu, asthma, coughs, colds, fever, and sciatica.' It is hard to believe that one plant could treat so many different conditions. Probably there was a placebo element involved.

Illnesses which do not seem to have been treated with herbal remedies were major killers like plague and smallpox. On 28th October 1770, the minister of

Kirkoswald read the King's order in Privy Council for preventing the plague from Danzig (modern Gdansk).[15] No further details were recorded and although the last outbreak of the plague in Ayr was in the previous century, there was certain to have been great anxiety about the possibility of its return, particularly since Ayr continued to trade with the Baltic.

Small–pox was a major cause of concern in the eighteenth century. The minister of Ballantrae 'lamented that inoculation for the small–pox is not more practised.'[16] In Girvan the report stated, 'there is still in this parish a considerable prejudice against inoculation,'[17] but in Mauchline, 'inoculation for the smallpox is practised with success.'[18] The Old Cumnock report reads:

> An aversion to inoculation prevails here, and has not yet been removed by all the pains made use of; in consequence of this smallpox makes havoc among the children. But this must gradually lessen, as inoculation gains ground, though slowly every year.[19]

Muirkirk,[20] Symington,[21] and Sorn,[22] all reported problems in promoting inoculation, the latter providing an explanation for the difficulty:

> The smallpox indeed, commits the same ravages here as in other places where inoculation is not generally practised. The notions of absolute pre–destination, which are still deeply rooted in the minds of the country people, lead the generality of them to look upon inoculation as implying as impious distrust of Divine Providence and vain attempt to alter irreversible decrees.

In this Sorn report, the minister went on to relate the loss of six children, and to commend three families who had their children successfully inoculated as was general in the village of Catrine. He hoped that these examples would help to remove the remaining prejudices. By the time of the *New Statistical Account,* Dalrymple[23] reported one case in eight years, Dalmellington[24] that the estimated time for the return of the disease was from seven to ten years; otherwise smallpox was not commented upon. However, there was smallpox in Ayr in 1856 and again in 1874 when 19 cases were reported.[25] Although the victims of smallpox were mainly children, in many cases their parents were, or had been, servants and had they lived, the children too would have become servants in due course.

In 1832, there was a major outbreak of cholera in Ayr with 79 deaths resulting from the 229 cases.[26] Thirty patients were admitted to a hospital set up in a church in Wallacetown, and 24 relatives of infected persons were admitted to a House of Seclusion. Vagrants and other suspects were banned from the town, tar barrels and torches burned day and night, and those who could fled the town. A further serious outbreak of cholera occurred in Ayr in 1849.[27]

In 1817, the Ayr, Newton and Wallacetown Dispensary was started to administer 'medical advice and relief gratuitously to all labouring under disease, or requiring surgical aid, whose means could not enable them to pay the usual fees of a medical practitioner.' Subscribers to the Dispensary could nominate one patient per year. Treatment was provided by the five medical men of the town and was available to more than 500 families. Cow–pox inoculations were given, and when necessary patients could be visited in their own houses.[28]

A small Fever Hospital was opened in Ayr in 1844 following an epidemic of typhus in 1841, when there were 211 cases within a couple of months. It was not until 1875 that this began to function as a General Hospital and to receive patients from all parts of the county.[29]

Apart from these epidemic diseases, the major fatal disease which those of working age were likely to contract was consumption (pulmonary tuberculosis), or scrofula (tuberculosis of the lymphatic glands), sometimes recorded as 'king's evil'. Since tuberculin testing of cattle was not introduced into the West of Scotland until the 1950s and many farm servants had daily contact with dairy animals and their products, it is perhaps not surprising that tuberculosis was so common.

Throughout the period covered by this study, it was expected that people should be self–reliant and not become a charge on public or charitable funds. The concept of retirement as it is viewed today was unknown and people could expect to work at whatever they were able to do or seek assistance from their families or friends. The poor law records and census returns cite numerous examples of elderly people who supported themselves by such tasks as 'winding pirns' for weavers, sewing, washing, making besoms (brooms) or doing casual field work.

The Registers of Deaths for Ayr from March 1766 to May 1820[30] show very few servants, and for Dailly, from 1802–1812,[31] no occupations at all are given. It is very likely that many of the women had spent part of their lives in service, although they were listed simply as 'wife of' or 'relict of.' Another possibility is that servants who developed serious illnesses may have been returned to their own family to be cared for, which might have been in a neighbouring parish. Also, in the eighteenth and early nineteenth century it was not compulsory to register a death, and the people most likely to be omitted from any register were the servants. Sometimes employers marked the passing of a long serving and valued servant by erecting a head stone as these examples show:

> Er[ected] by JOHN RITCHIE of Aringa Australia in mem[ory] of his nurse MARGARET RONALDSON who was for 35 years a faithful and respected servant in Tarbolton Manse, where she died at an advanced age 11 Mar 18[3]5.[32]

Thos Burnie 21. 2. 1855 76, (for) the period of 46 years butler in Blairquhan.[33]

Mrs Charlotte Robinson 1.1855. 94. Faithful servant in the Kilkerran and Bargany families for more than half a century.[34]

These examples were exceptional, and the vast majority of servants would have been interred in unmarked graves.

Savings and Insurance

In the eighteenth century, a person who had money to spare could lend it to another individual who needed it, in return for a promissory note to return the money with interest by a given date. Failure to settle the debt could lead to imprisonment. Ayr tolbooth housed all kinds of prisoners, including debtors. Sometimes, the pursuer seeking to have a dept repaid was a servant, for example, '23 February 1762 Margaret Howie indweller in Ayr and John Jamieson her son were incarcerated within the tolbooth in Ayr . . . owing by them to John MacKintosh Servant to John Smith in Killoch in the Parish of Mauchline . . .'[35]

In August 1768, William and Robert Harris were incarcerated in the tolbooth of Ayr for forging 'twenty shilling banknotes.'[36] The collapse of the Ayr Bank (1769–1772) led to 'a general rush to cash notes.'[37] But it was unlikely that the labouring classes held accounts with the Ayr Bank; rather that their wages had been paid in bank notes because of the shortage of coin in Scotland at that time, or even because it was fashionable to have paper money.

In the nineteenth century, great emphasis was placed on self–reliance as a virtue to be encouraged. The institution of local savings banks provided the opportunity for members of the servant class to accumulate modest savings.

The *Air Advertiser* of 16th March 1815 printed the news that:

The Directors of the Bank of Scotland, being desirous of giving encouragement to the establishment of PARISH BANKS, for the SAVINGS of the POOR over SCOTLAND, have authorised their Agents to give Five per Cent on all sums that may be lodged at any of the Agencies on that account.[38]

Two weeks later, a further intimation in the same newspaper confirmed that the local magistrates and ministers had agreed to the establishment of the bank for the parishes of Ayr, Newton and St. Quivox, '[t]he object being to induce the deposit of small savings that a Bank will not take and which otherwise might be squandered away.'[39]

On 4th May 1815, The *Air Advertiser* stated:

We are happy to find, that the SAVINGS BANK, established by the Provost, Magistrates and a number of Gentlemen in the neighbourhood, is to be opened on Monday first, and we trust the labouring classes of the community will avail themselves of it, and that it will be followed with consequences truly beneficial –*See Ad.*

ADVERTISEMENT   THE SAVINGS or PROVIDENT BANK for The Parishes of AIR, NEWTON and ST.QUIVOX, will be opened on MONDAY, at the Assembly Rooms, Air, betwixt the hours of Nine and Ten o'clock in the forenoon, to receive the earnings of Tradesmen, Labourers, Mechanics, Servants, &c. No sum less than One Shilling will be received. It is under the direction of Richard Alex, Oswald, Esq, Governor of the Institution, William Cowan, Esq. Deputy–Governor, Hugh Cowan, Esq. Treasurer, Thomas McClelland, Esq. Secretary. [The twelve directors were then listed] Air, 27th April, 1815.[40]

According to the *New Statistical Account,* the Ayr Savings Bank was modelled on that pioneered by the Rev Dr Duncan of Ruthwell.[41] It was promoted by William Cowan, a director of Cowan's Bank in Ayr and at that time Provost of the burgh. Deposits could range from 1s to £10, but when the account held £10, the depositor had to withdraw the sum and 'dispose of it elsewhere.'[42] This measure ensured that large depositors could not avail themselves of the favourable interest rate provided for small savers. Over the years, the rate of interest had varied. Cowan's Bank was taken over in 1831,[43] and by 1837 Hunter's Bank in which the savings bank deposits were then lodged was allowing ½% more than the current rate of interest, the Savings Bank being then located in the Kirk Port, with Adam M'Hutcheon listed as treasurer and Wm. Cowan Jun. Secretary.[44] From its inception until 1842, both accounts and the amount of money on deposit seem to have grown progressively (see table). The following year Hunter's Bank itself was taken over by the Union Bank.[45] The history of Ayr Savings Bank between 1843 and its revival in 1909 would require further research.[46]

The Rev. Alexander Cuthill in his *New Statistical Account* report noted that:

A great proportion of the depositors consist of apprentices and servant girls, who are thus inured to habits of economy, prudence, and foresight, while they lay up in store besides, a small fund, which they will find of incalculable advantage for their future establishment in life, either in the way of marriage or of trade.

He saw the Savings Bank as a means of protecting the young from 'thoughtless follies and excesses' and of preventing the old from 'becoming a burden on their friends or the public.'[47] The Rev. James Stevenson of Newton–upon–Ayr reported of the Ayr Savings Bank, '[t]he depositors in general belong to the various classes of mechanics, weavers, masons, shoemakers, carpenters, &c.– and a very considerable proportion are females, employed in needlework, or as domestic servants.'[48] It would be interesting to know how the depositors were able to spare the time on Monday morning to visit the bank and whether, since the majority of servants were paid twice yearly, most of the deposits were made on the Mondays following the May and November terms, and withdrawals made less frequently, possibly only when debts were pressing or when sickness or unemployment necessitated.

The Mauchline Savings Bank was established in 1815 and by 1837, 'the deposits of investors mostly from the labouring classes amount to £900, the sums annually invested about £140, while nearly as much is withdrawn.'[49] By 1844 it had ceased to exist.[50]

The parish of Dailly had a savings bank, founded in 1817,[51] and still in existence in 1844.[52] In 1837 it had almost £700 on deposit but by then annual withdrawals were exceeding the deposits being made. It held the remaining life savings of some old people, and other depositors according to the report were:

> farm servants, labourers, colliers, females who live by their needle, children in whose names parents have entered small sums on security for their having something wherewith to educate them, or send them out into the world. The treasurers of the friendly societies also lodge their spare cash in the savings bank.[53]

A savings bank that started in Barr in 1819, 'has proved of considerable benefit to servants and labourers, for whom it is exclusively designed. It has suffered, however, from the pressure of the times within the last two or three years, and the sum now deposited does not exceed £150.'[54] Barr Savings Bank ceased its operations in 1844.[55]

The parishioners of Dundonald, which included the town of Troon, used the Irvine Savings Bank,[56] founded in 1815, whose depositors 'consist mostly of industrious mechanics and servants.'[57] Its annual report in January 1862 recorded 556 depositors with £1959 1s 1d on deposit.[58]

Under the patronage of the Marquess of Bute, the Cumnock Savings Bank was established in 1831 and directed by heritors and the ministers of Old Cumnock, New Cumnock and Auchinleck, the treasurer being Mr. Campbell, the schoolmaster of Old Cumnock. The Rev. Ninian Ballantyne reported:

> The stock on the first of January 1836 amounted to £810, deposits from that date till 2d January 1837, were £421 9s 4½d; the sums drawn out during that period, £251 9s 4½d: accumulated stock on 2d January 1837, £980. The number of depositors during the year was 223; and they consist, for the most part of male and female servants, though there is also a number of trades people among them.[59]

By 1844, it seems that Old Cumnock had two Savings Banks, one having 606 depositors and the other 232 depositors.[60] Few of the inhabitants of Auchinleck used the Cumnock banks, but in 1841, 116 depositors from Sorn did, and in 1842 the number had increased to 173.[61] It is likely that workers from the Catrine cotton mill used this branch.

Maybole Savings Bank was established in May 1831, and catered for the town and the adjacent villages. The 1837 *New Statistical Account* report provides an interesting breakdown of its depositors:

	Male	Female	Total
farm–servants	26	44	70
domestic servants			25
sewers etc.			46
children etc.			47
labourers			28
weavers etc.			25
mechanics etc.			17
not classed			15
Totals	**126**	**147**	**273**

The amount held on deposit at this time was £1152 14s.[62] By the end of 1842, the number of depositors had fallen to 103.[63] Between 1831 and 1837, 36 male tradesman and servants, and 27 female sewers and servants from Dalrymple used the Maybole Savings Bank. On average they invested yearly £73 and withdrew £41.[64] This branch no longer existed in 1844.[65] The Straiton branch of the Maybole Savings Bank was not very successful, the provident servants preferring 'to open an account for themselves in Ayr.'[66] Kirkmichael's two savings banks had 'very little in.'[67] Ochiltree's bank, also founded in 1831, was 'found to be a great benefit to trades people, farm–servants &c.',[68] but by 1844, 'the funds are not on the increase.'[69] Dalmellington Savings Bank, founded in 1834, had between £200 and £300 on deposit in 1836,[70] the depositors being 'chiefly young workmen and servants.' By 1844, it did not exist.[71] Girvan reported 60 depositors in 1842, and 87 in 1843.[72] Tarbolton had a savings bank in 1842,[73] which was still operational in 1844,[74] but no details are available.

The operation of these small savings banks depended upon the voluntary work of the treasurers and trustees who ran them, but in September 1861, the Post Office Savings Bank was established, paying interest to small savers of 2½%, and by early in 1862, the POSB had opened in every county in Scotland.[75]

At some point in the eighteenth century, friendly societies were founded to protect their members and their families in the event of sickness, old age and death or sometimes unemployment. Writing in 1791, the Rev. William Auld mentions the Mauchline Friendly Society which was established about ten years before, and which 'allowed 2/– per week for those unable to work and 3/– for those confined to bed.' There was an entry fee of one guinea and it had a current stock of £300.[76] The Tarbolton report of 1796 reads: 'here is a farmer society for the purposes of the friendly societies now common in Scotland.'[77] Probably these two societies did not have servant members, but many farmers started their careers as farm servants and sent their sons and daughters to serve on other farms, so there may have been some indirect benefit. The same may be said of Mutual Support, founded in Ayr in 1796,[78] and the Muirkirk Friendly Society commenced on 3rd July 1790.[79]

In 1815 the *Air Advertiser* reported that in December 1804 the Countess of Crawfurd and 'a few benevolent Ladies in the town and neighbourhood'[80] had founded a friendly society to cater for up to 45 women between 40 and 65 years whose ages precluded them from eligibility for joining the other female societies. Each woman had to pay an entry fee, plus 'one penny per week or 4s 6d yearly, including twopence to the officer'. The report continued:

> The Society held their tenth general meeting on Monday last, and the good it has done will be best shown, by stating the sum given annually to the sick, from amongst the forty–five general members, which has been as follows;

the year		the year	
1805	£4 18 0	1810	£32 6 6
1806	13 16 6	1811	43 6 6
1807	21 5 0	1812	41 19 0
1808	18 11 0	1813	45 18 0
1809	30 18 0	1814	56 5 0

> The Society has now in stock £345. Another proof of the utility of benefit societies.

A copy of the rules of this society was deposited with the Ayr Burgh Records and is appended here [Appendix 3]. Lady Lilias Oswald, wife of the local member of parliament and niece of the Countess of Crawfurd, was the patroness of a similarly funded female society, 'to which the ordinary members pay a regular quarterly assessment of 1s 2d and receive an aliment of 4s per week in sickness, besides an allowance for marriage and funeral expenses.'[81] This friendly society had a membership of 150 in 1844.[82] Between 1796 and 1836, fifteen named friendly societies were founded in Ayr.[83] By 1844, these fifteen societies had a total membership of 1626.[84] Unfortunately, it is not possible to match the names of the societies given in the *New Statistical Account of Scotland* to the breakdown of membership numbers given in the *Appendix* to *the 1844 Poor Law Report*. It is also difficult to decide whether some of the societies listed for Newton–upon–Ayr and for St. Quivox are in addition to those given for Ayr, or whether they drew their membership from all three parishes.

Girvan had 11 societies with a membership of 60–80 each, and a female society membership of 70.[85] Maybole had six societies founded between 1796 and 1825. Their titles, Love and Unity, Philanthropic, Caledonian, Social and Humane, Albion, Benevolent Love and Unity Female,[86] gave little indication of the occupations of their members. Cumnock and Mauchline each had three friendly societies with memberships in each parish below 300, whereas Sorn, which included Catrine Cotton Mill, had a membership of 104 in its female society, and 273 in its male society.[87] Most of the smaller villages had one or more friendly societies.

There can be little doubt that these various societies were established with the best of intentions, and many of them must have provided much needed assistance to their members. However, those that were not funded by patrons were prone to run into difficulties. When a large proportion of the membership became old, or when an epidemic illness caused multiple sickness and death, the outgoings of the society would exceed the income, and the society would no longer be viable.

For many, the Penny Savings Bank fulfilled a need and there were such banks in Annbank, Dalrymple and Maybole, the history of the latter being particularly well documented. It was started in the West Church, Maybole, in October 1866, shortly after the Rev. Roderick Lawson began his ministry there, and although very successful, ceased in 1893, because no volunteers came forward to act as trustees when he retired. As he wrote in his newsletter of December 1892, 'the difficulty as the Trustees lies in the annual auditing of some 700 separate Pass–book Accounts, which it will be no small work to collect.'[88]

The business of this Penny Bank was conducted on a Monday evening, and although started for the children of the parish, it grew to cater for the whole town. It was administered by the minister himself, aided by an assistant, and over the years was conducted at several different locations. In his newsletter of October 1886, the minister recalled how 'a field–worker laid down 16s with the remark, "I've tried to save *in a stocking* but can't manage it, sae I'll *try you*."[89] Summing up his work with the bank he wrote:

> I have failed in many things, but not in this. I have helped to make homes happier, and lives more comfortable. I have helped some to buy houses, others to emigrate to more prosperous lands, others to begin business, and many to commence a habit which is not to be valued by their savings alone, but by a habit of self denial which will live and work as long as life endures.[90]

These various means by which the servant class were encouraged to save did much to reduce their demands on public funds or on the charity of the members of society.

Furthermore, although the savings of the individual might be small, the accumulated savings of the entire class must have provided a substantial investment both in the local and national economy.

Year	Deposits	Accounts
1822	£1100	358
1828	£1700	448
1829	£1844	524
1830	£1696	535
1831	£1536	526
1832	£1533	511
1833	£1785	564
1834	£1738	559
1835	£2325	604
1836	£2686	684
1837	£3320	700
1838		702
1839		775
1840		770
1841		834
1842		824

Table 1. Ayr Savings Bank Deposits & Accounts, 1822–1842. Table compiled from *The New Statistical Account of Scotland* and the *Appendix to the Report of the Poor Law*, 1844.

Poverty

Although there has never been a good time to be poor, the majority in the first years of the twenty–first century can have no conception of what it meant to be poor in earlier times. Before the 1845 Poor Law came into force, each parish was responsible for the care for its own sick and needy parishioners. Funds were raised by church collections, fines, the hire of mort cloths for funerals, interest received from legacies or from money lent to a landowner, donations from heritors, and from special collections.

The Scottish Poor Law acknowledged four classes of poor, these being: the 'ordinary poor' including the aged and infirm, those requiring temporary help because of illness or bereavement, the unemployed, and vagrants and beggars.

Whereas aid would be given to the ordinary poor and those needing limited help for a short time, the unemployed particularly if able bodied were often refused assistance. Vagrants were treated as criminals but some beggars might be given a badge which allowed them to beg within the parish of residence. None of these badges seem to have survived locally, although they are mentioned in kirk session records. Probably they were similar to those now held in Dunblane museum.

The Ayr Poorhouse was opened in 1756, and one of its rules was that girls who were fit were to be employed by the mistress 'in washing house–clothes and in doing other kitchen duties.' She was also to teach them to spin and to 'train them for service.' Thirty years later, the directors advertised that, 'they had several boys in the Poorhouse of age suitable for apprenticeship, as well as girls fitted for service.'[91]

The Poor Law (Scotland) Amendment Act 1845 introduced a new system of poor relief, which was only replaced in 1948. It set up a Board of Supervision with a Parochial Board of Management for each burgh or combination of parishes, empowered to raise funds by assessment, half to be paid by the landowners and half by the tenants. These boards were required to compile a roll of those entitled to relief, appoint inspectors of the poor and administer the funds. Inspectors had to visit and personally inspect all claimants twice or more during the year. Provision was made for these boards to erect poorhouses. In south Ayrshire, Ayr Poorhouse was replaced by Kyle Union Poorhouse in 1860, and Maybole Poorhouse by Maybole Combination Poorhouse in 1865. Cumnock had a poorhouse until 1886, but it sent 'some cases to Ayr Poorhouse or to the asylums.'[92] Claimants from Ballantrae and Colmonell had to seek relief from the board in Stranraer. Whereas in former times poor relief was regarded as a charity by both the givers and the recipients, it now became more controlled and systematic with prescriptive rules set, although permitting persons dissatisfied with their treatment to lodge their complaints with the board of supervision.

Poorhouse inmates were not allowed to make any noise when ordered to be silent, revile or insult any person by either word or deed, threaten to strike or assault any person, refuse or neglect work, pretend sickness, play cards or other games of chance, enter premises allocated to another class of inmate, behave improperly at public worship or prayers, fail to cleanse themselves, remain outwith the poorhouse beyond the time given for their temporary leave of absence or 'wilfully disobey any lawful order of any officer of the poorhouse.'[93] Infringement of any of these general rules could be deemed 'disorderly' and, as such, could be punished by requiring one or two hours extra work for either one or two days during which time all butter and milk was to be withheld from the offender's meals. No doubt some of these rules were necessary for the welfare of the majority of the residents, but others seem to have been designed to deter people from seeking relief. Indeed, 'admission to the poorhouse was often offered as a test of whether an applicant was genuine.'[94] The inspector's report on Kyle Union Poorhouse dated 7th September 1869 supports this view: 'the dissolute classes should not receive the indulgence of liberty as the value of the test is thereby diminished.'[95]

In Kyle Union Poorhouse, the day began at 6 a.m. in summer and 7 a.m. in winter. Children went to bed at 8 p.m. and adults at 9 p.m. when all lights were extinguished. Straw was used for bedding, being replaced in April 1861 by sprit, a coarse reedy rush or grass grown on marshy ground and sometimes used in rope–making and stack thatching. In November the following year, rye straw was used for the bedding. Price and availability probably governed the material used.

The beds had to be tidied in the regulation manner in the mornings, and made up for use in the evening. In August 1880, the inspector recommended two sheets per bed as an economy to avoid too frequent scouring of blankets, to which the committee agreed. He also recommended that children should sleep in separate beds, partly to control the spread of head lice, but the committee considered this would incur 'unnecessary expenditure' for 'in the case of children of the working class and in many other instances, separate beds for each child was unknown. Besides children in the house would most likely sleep in couples not withstanding their having separate beds.'

Breakfast was served at 9 a.m., dinner at 2 p.m. and supper at 6 p.m. For breakfast and supper, the prescribed diet for adults of both sexes who were working, was 4 ounces of meal with 3 gills of milk. For dinner they were entitled to 8 ounces of bread, $1\frac{1}{2}$ pints of broth and 4 ounces of boiled meat. In October 1860 the governor was given permission to substitute potatoes for bread, the potatoes to be grown by the inmates.

In April 1862, it was left to the governor to decide whether 'respectable persons' could attend Church in their own clothes, but in September of the same year, the committee ruled that all inmates must attend Church in the house clothes.

Friends and relatives were allowed to visit on Fridays between 10 a.m. and 2 p.m. They could bring gifts such as tea, but no alcohol. Permission could be granted at the discretion of the governor and the visiting committee for inmates to leave the house for a short time, with the requirement that young girls were to be chaperoned to prevent them having access to alcohol. Smoking was banned from all the rooms and was only permitted at all when specially allowed by the governor and the surgeon. The governor could allow or withhold tea, snuff or tobacco as a means of enforcing discipline.

The use of privies (dry toilets) was restricted during the day and water closets were locked in the daytime except in the sick wards. In 1882, two baths were installed on the upper floor, one for males and one for females, but it was considered too expensive to fit hot water pipes, so hot water had to be carried up from the wash house. Four years later, the drains had to be inspected following an outbreak of typhoid.

The poorhouse and its gravel–covered airing yards were surrounded by high walls. Doors between the various parts of the house were locked thus separating family members from each other. The only recorded relief from what appears to have been a miserable existence for the inmates was a holiday to Dalmellington in 1863, presumably a day trip, and the supply of ale at Christmas in 1871.

In order to receive relief, applicants had to establish a right to claim by virtue of birthplace (in the case of married women, their husband's birthplace), or three years' settlement, the latter being especially difficult for those who frequently changed their place of service. When applicants had to return to their parishes of settlement, they could claim a night's lodging from the parishes through which they passed. Since Maybole Combination Poorhouse was on the main road from Portpatrick to the north, it had to provide lodgings for transients as follows:[96]

Year	Number	Year	Number
1855	96	1860	127
1856	171	1861	245
1857	161	1862	320
1858	191	1863	77
1859	172		

The numbers for 1863 were the result of a new regime when many applicants were refused. The record of applications for relief, many of whom were of the servant class, make sad reading as the following examples show:

9.30 p.m. 9 July 1855, Margaret Robertson or Graham a 29 year old servant, born in Scotland, with residence in Perth and her children, David aged 3 years and Adam 3 months. Deserted by her husband whom she thinks is in the Militia. Offered lodging for the night.

6 p.m. 25 Nov. 1856, Catherine Murdoch, a 30 year old single, washerwomen, born in Scotland, with illegitimate children, James Wright aged 4 who appears to be dying and Janet Wright aged 7 weeks. James Wright, the children's father is in jail for stealing a pair of boots from his master. Relief given.

11 p.m. 23 Sept. 1858, Elizabeth McMurtrie, 64, a single servant, 'who can sew a white seam'. Except a short time that she was chargeable in Barony [Glasgow], Elizabeth has supported herself by service and taking care of an old couple who are dead, Doctor certifies 'an inward complaint'. Offered relief.

7p.m. 14 May 1862, Peter Frazer, a 37 year old Widower, a Servant to Gentleman, native of Dundee, and his children, Isabel 7 and Jessie 4. Given lodging for the night.

Noon, 7 Oct. 1862, Catherine Dunlop, a single, 17 year old servant, with 8 hour old female child. Mother a pauper. Catherine given temporary relief.

The conditions in Maybole Combination and Kyle Union Poorhouses were similar, as each was obliged to conform to national standard. On 27th August 1866, the governor at Maybole reported that, 'a female inmate had got out of the house by one of the windows on the ground floor and been in communication with her friends over the boundary wall.' He suggested that 'a lockfast gate should be erected on each of the two stairs leading to the second floor' in order to prevent a repetition of the offence, and the board accepted this suggestion.[97] It would appear that containing the inmates was more important than fire safety precautions in this case.

When older applicants applied for relief every attempt was made to require their working sons and daughters, often in service, to contribute to the support of their elderly or infirm parents. Living conditions in the poorhouse were basic, but most humiliating was the loss of all dignity and freedom, yet for the not inconsiderable number of servants who suffered misfortune, that was what necessity forced upon them.

Crime and Punishment

Crime and punishment are common features of all societies and have been throughout the ages, though considerable variations can be seen in what has constituted a crime and the type and degree of punishment imposed upon those deemed guilty.

Smuggling, or the attempted evasion of duties imposed on designated goods, has existed for centuries, but has varied according to the type of goods subject to tax, the demand for their supply and the possibility of outwitting government officials appointed to collect the duty money. Eighteenth century Ayrshire was notorious for the smuggling trade, and all classes of society were likely to have been involved either directly or indirectly. The goods dealt in were mainly salt, tea, tobacco, brandy and silks.

In August 1750, an unmarried servant women, Agnes Maclauchlin, daughter of Robert Maclauchlin, Dailly, 'was sent by the family at Dalwhirr to see if Thomas Campbell would grind some meil for their use.'[98] According to the miller, his wife 'was attending on her mother near Girvan.' The following January, Agnes appeared before Dailly Kirk Session, 'acknowledged herself with child' to Thomas Campbell, which he denied. On 5th April 1751, he was committed to the Tolbooth of Ayr on a smuggling charge, and in October the same year, the Lords of Justiciary ordered him to be transported to America. Agnes was disciplined by the kirk session for adultery. She and Campbell's wife were presumably left to manage as best they could.

As mentioned in Chapter 1, on 16th June 1765, Kirkoswald Kirk Session was dealing with what appeared to be a routine case of 'the sin of Fornication before Marriage' when they were informed that the defendant, Samuel Brown had also violated a Sabbath Day during the previous October. He declared that he had attended the Church that day and afterwards, he had gone to the shore where he saw the vessel with 'counterband goods' come in, and having been ordered to guard the unloaded goods on the shore by Archibald Ritchie, Commander of the King's wherry, he did so, and played no further part in the affair.[99] He was required to acknowledge the offence, show sorrow, and never to repeat the transgression. The session was anxious to know if others had also profaned the Sabbath and made inquiries, which led to the naming of a further 46 persons, which included:

> Andrew Ross Cottar in Ardlochan and confessed that he Imployed said Lord's Day in Carrying Ankors of Spirits out of the water unto the Shore, and that he Declares that he was Compell'd unto this by Mr Ritchie Commander of the Kings Boat.

> John Carnochan in Old Mill of Jamieson and confess'd before the Session, that among others was upon the Shore upon the above Day, and having staid a while, and as he was Returning home, he Met two Manx Men who Delivered to him an Anker of Spirits, which he carried home to his House, and Kept it all night, and Delivered it again to them next Morning.

> Elizabeth Brown Servant in Ardlochan. She Confess'd that she was upon the shore the above Night, and carried one Casque out of the sea, and kept it in her Custody all night and Restored it Next Day.

> Hugh McClure, Servant in Leigh Drumdow and confess'd he went part of the way to the shore upon the above Night, with Horses.

The confessions of all those who appeared before the session provide a graphic picture of a smuggling run which encountered difficulties. It seems to have involved most of the adult population in that quarter of the parish either as participants or onlookers, yet the session showed no concern whatsoever for the law of the land being infringed, only that the Sabbath had been profaned. This incident must have been one of many where illegal trade involved a large section of the population of this coastal parish. In 1792, the Reverend Matthew Biggar reported that the change for the better in the standard of living and dress which had taken place throughout the country had happened earlier in Kirkoswald than in the neighbouring parishes. He thought it likely that this could be attributed to the prevalence of smuggling because those engaged in that activity dealt with foreign suppliers of tea, spirits and silks, and were in their turn able to provide 'their family and friends the means of greater luxury and finery, at the cheapest rate.'[100] Undoubtedly, many of the servant class would receive some benefit from this illegal trade, either because their labour was required to help carry or hide contraband goods, or because a payment in coin or kind could help to buy their silence.

However, when the eighteenth century black economy declined, local prosperity was affected. The minister of Girvan reported 'habits of regular industry were probably prevented or destroyed by the practice of smuggling, to which the inhabitants were for a long time so much addicted.'[101] The report from Straiton, a hilly parish some thirteen miles inland from both Girvan and Ayr, where there had been a considerable number of smugglers before the extension of the excise laws, was even more explicit for it claimed that the new regulations had resulted in increased risk, diminution of profits, marked decline in the smuggling trade, reduction of several previously prosperous families to poverty and the expectation of an increase in the number of poor.[102]

Because of the gains that could be made from smuggling, ruthless actions could be taken. On 5th March 1767, an attempt was made to murder Mr. Gordon, Surveyor and acting Comptroller of Customs at Ayr, and by 23rd April, 75 people had been examined and descriptions and sheriff's warrants issued in respect of 'four servants of notorious smugglers in the parish of Dundonald', who had been involved in 'the plot to waylay and murder Mr. Gordon.' To avoid incriminating the chief culprit they had left their service and the county.[103] They were:

> Mathew Reid, servant to Robert Fulton in Corraith, twenty–seven years of age, tall stature, black complexion, with his own hair tied and born in the parish of Symington.

> William Strachan, servant to David Dunlop in Schullochmiln, twenty years of age, middle stature, black complexion, with his own black hair and born in the parish of Monkton.

> James Gray, servant to James Vallance in Loans twenty years of age, middle stature, black complexion, and his own black hair and born in the parish of Monkton.

> David Hunter, servant to Robert Allison in Corrieth and working in Willowston, twenty years of age, low stature, brown complexion pitted with small pox, wearing his own red hair and born in the parish of Prestwick.

The Collector of Customs at Ayr reported to the Board of Excise in Edinburgh, 'we are told they went on board a sloop or cutter after her cargo was run at Troon Point and are gone to France or Ireland, no doubt at the desire of their masters and others concerned in the plot to defeat the discovery of their crimes.'

The extent of the smuggling operation at Troon was considerable, numerous boats were involved and the Collector at Ayr claimed to have been well informed that after goods had been landed, 'about five hundred horses have often been got thither in an hour's warning to carry them away to different places in the country.'

He wanted 'to put a stop to the illegal trade carried on by almost the whole inhabitants of the parish of Dundonald' and was able to report, 'Happily the commutation act has nearly annihilated the hostile trade.'[104] He commented, 'It must be acknowledged that lessening some duties to a certain degree would not injure revenue; and yet more effectively cut up this business, than a fleet of cutters, or an army of custom and excise officers.' A similar situation prevailed in Ayr parish where the minister wrote, 'the people in general are humane and charitable, live comfortably, and are contented with their circumstances. Their morals in many instances have suffered by the practice of smuggling, which is not yet entirely suppressed in this place.'[105]

Tastes change over time, and brandy was superseded by whisky which was smuggled into Ayr from Arran. An agent for this illegal activity was a woman known as Aunt Bettie. She kept a boarding house in 'what was considered an aristocratical portion of Newton – Garden Street.'[106] She had been 'a servant in genteel houses and only become married at an age when frequently women become widows.' The annual midsummer fair provided an excellent opportunity for Arran men to visit and replenish her stock. She was well known amongst the more respectable class of people, and supplied the *Shirra* [sheriff] and most of the Court officials, as well as the gentry of Wellington Square, with 'bead–twenty–two.'

If smuggling was a crime that could involve all sections of society, vagrancy was confined to an underclass of 'the undeserving poor.' An entry in Dailly Kirk Session records dated 29th May 1752 refers to two acts of the Justices of the Peace regarding the poor and vagrancy. Vagrants were 'under pain of being apprehended by the constable and incarcerated in the prison of Ayr and fed on bread and water for ten days . . .'[107] It would seem that the enforcement of these acts was somewhat variable for, on the one hand the 'Register of Incarcerations, Liberations, Arrestments & Loosings Thereof' for the Burgh of Ayr records the names of vagrants who were incarcerated in the Tolbooth, and on the other the *[Old] Statistical Account* report for Kirkoswald deplored the hoards 'of Irish vagrants & beggars who travel the great post road from Ayr to Port Patrick.'[108] It condemned the harassing of the many farmers living close to the road and desired 'the police of the country to remedy the evil.'

As might be expected a vagrant could also be found guilty of theft, as for example 'Parlan McFarlane a vagrant . . . having stolen an apron or Towell out of a house and who was incarcerated on 17th Decr. 1768.'[109] Punishment for theft could be harsher, as in the case of Mary McNeill, who was imprisoned in the Tolbooth of Ayr on 2nd November 1753, whipped through the town by the common hangman, then recommitted to the Tolbooth, 'to Remain till she is Liberate in Due Course of Law for the Crime of Stealing Cloaths and of virtue of warrand from the justices of the peace mett at their quarter sessions of Ayr the Thirtyth October Last.'

Perhaps a more unusual case of theft was that committed by Elizabeth Maxwell alias Euphan Maxwell, an old servant of James Gibson, vintner in Ayr. She was incarcerated on 15th October 1753, because on Saturday night 6th October or Sunday Morning 7th October, 'James Gibson's house was Broke open where the locks of a press and pantry were taken off and taken furth of said press some money and taken furth of said pantry, two silver spoons and some other things.' While still employed by James Gibson she had been found guilty of theft, imprisoned and released. He suspected her of this second crime and when she was apprehended, she was found to have a pair of his wife's stockings. She confessed to having stolen the money amounting to nineteen shillings which she swallowed to conceal the theft. Eighteen pence of this money was found on her person. She further confessed to having stolen two silver spoons which she threw into the well of James Gibson's Close. A search was made and these were recovered.[110]

Some of the saddest crimes were those of the young women who were arrested for child murder. In 1690, an act was passed 'anent Muthering Children' which required that,

> if any woman shall conceal her Child, during the whole Space, and shall not call for and make use of help and Assistance in the Birth, the Child being found dead or Missing, the Mother shall be holden and Reputed the Mutherer of her own Child. And ordains all Criminal Judges to Sustain such process, and the Libel being remitted to the Knowledge of an Inquest, it shall be sufficient Ground for them to Return their Verdict finding the Libel proven and the Mother guilty of Muther, tho' there be No Appearance of wound or Bruise upon the Body of the Child.[111]

In 1762, an Act of the General Assembly of the Church of Scotland required that the above act should be read from the pulpit of each parish church at least twice a year.[112] Despite the publicity given to this crime, some women must have seen it as the only solution to their predicament. On 21st February 1760, 'Jean Wood latly servant' was accused, 'of having brought furth a Child without Discovering her being with child or calling the Assistance at the time of birth and the child being found dead.'[113] Four days later she died in prison. Christine Kerr was accused of Child Murder on 27th August 1767 and on 8th September sentence was passed 'that Captain Brown Shipmaster in Liverpool should Transport and land said Christine Kerr in one or other of his Majesties Plantations in America Agreeable to and in terms of a Sentence of Banishment pronounced by the said Circuit.'[114]

Each of the burghs had its own jail. In Maybole, there was the old Tolbooth where for hundreds of years crimes from murder to poaching were dealt with.[115] From 1804 to 1839, the JP court in Cumnock met in the old parish school with the jail attached, the latter measuring 12 feet long and 22 feet wide.[116] So either there were few prisoners at any one time or they were very cramped for space. The parish church building which stood in Cumnock from 1754 to 1866 had jougs fastened to one of the outside walls,[117] by which means an offender, wearing an iron collar, could be shackled to the wall, and exposed to public vilification. Prestwick had a jail, largely for petty offenders, but where serious offenders could be held before being transferred to Ayr for trial before the Sheriff.[118]   In Girvan, 'The Old Jail, built in 1789, was a two story building with a thatched roof through which prisoners frequently made good their escape. It was known as stumpy.'[119] The present Stumpy Tower had prison cells on three floors and gave access to the Courtroom where the local Justices met to hear the cases.   Prisoners remained overnight in this jail and were transferred to Ayr the following day. In the 1870s a new jail was built.[120]   Prisoners entering the Tolbooth of Ayr, climbed the nineteen steps from the Sandgate, and passed through the guard–house to reach the rat–infested cells on the second floor.   There were four or six cells in addition to a debtors' room. 'The Court House occupied the third story, and the culprits below had the satisfaction of hearing the judges meeting above them and making diverse remarks on those who were to be tried for misdemeanours.'[121]

In the early 1820s, the new County Jail was built at the rear of the new County Buildings in Wellington Square, Ayr, where it stood for a century. A few years after it opened, a strict regime was initiated in the establishment.   Prisoners had to work from 6 a.m. to 8 p.m. daily.   They had to wash daily and keep their quarters clean and aired.

Younger men without a trade were taught to weave, older men had to pick oakum (*i.e.* to separate old rope into loose fibre), which was needed to caulk the hulls of sailing ships.   Women inmates had to undertake domestic chores to fit them for service on release.   In July 1837, the prison housed 16 males and 5 females with an annual turnover of 82.[122]

The Criminal Offenders (Scotland) Report for 1846 lists only 3 males and no females in Ayr Prison as having superior education out of a total of 96 male and 34 female offenders, so it seems probable that the majority of the prison population came from the lower orders.[123]   This does not imply that most servants were criminals; only that adverse circumstances could make them more vulnerable to falling foul of the law.

Leisure and Literacy

When consideration is given to the long hours which servants were required to work, and the low levels of monetary remuneration which they received, the opportunities for them to enjoy leisure activities must have been limited. Because of these limitations, there was probably a far higher value placed on simple pleasures than is often the case today, for peoples' aspirations must be limited by the availability of opportunities to fulfil them.

For the lower orders of society, the period from the eighteenth century to well into the nineteenth century was a time of transition from a purely oral culture to a semi–literate one. Whereas access to the written word was limited, the spoken word was universal, and servants would derive pleasure from gossiping or blethering about people and happenings around them.

Opportunities to gossip could often be made within the working day, as for instance when fetching water from the well. This was considered to be 'a nice job,' and it was said that some servants would not accept a situation unless they were engaged, among other duties, as the lass that 'was tae gang for the water.'[124] The Sandgate well in Ayr, and doubtless public wells in the other burghs and villages, were ideal venues for servants to converse with each other as they queued to fill their wooden pails or *stoups.*

Another opportunity for combining work and pleasure was a *rocking* when friends and neighbours would gather to spin or knit and at the same time entertain themselves. Such meetings would be held on moon–lit nights in spring or winter turn about in the local farm–houses.[125] Burns described one of these gatherings in his "Epistle to John Lapraik":

> On Fasten'en we had a rockin',
> To Ca' the crack and weave our stockin',
> And there was muckle fun and jokin',
> Ye need na doubt,
> At length we had a hearty yokin'
> At sing about.

In the eighteenth century farmhouses the servants who were probably the sons and daughters of other tenant farmers, could expect to be included in such a gathering. Indeed, the maids and daughters of the household would be expected to hold a *rock* or distaff with tow (carded wool or flax) attached, and to spin their yarn as they listened to and no doubt joined in the fireside entertainment. Stories and jokes would be told, word games played, rhymes recited and songs sung. When hand spinning died out, the expression, 'I am coming over with my rock' came to mean that a social call was to be made.[126] The women of the household and their visiting neighbours would often begin their spinning during daylight hours, and be joined by the men in the evening when their outside work was done. The maids would be expected to spin whenever they were not engaged in other duties. This would, no doubt, be a chance for the women to gossip and enjoy female company.

In the nineteenth century similar groups would engage in sewing Ayrshire whitework, thus of necessity combining work and pleasure.

Ayrshire was fortunate to have produced a bard who has left a legacy of what would otherwise have been a lost oral culture. One servant who fed the imagination of Burns was Betty Davidson, an old maid of his mother's, who had been married to a cousin of hers. She was a repository of local folk tales which, despite the efforts of the Kirk, were still part of the psyche of the rural population, who continued to observe many of the old customs. In a case investigated by Maybole Kirk Session in 1780, Robert Pettigrew, a nineteen year old witness, testified that he and John McNeal were so late in the kitchen because they 'came in to get some salt cakes bak'd it being fastens even.'[127] According to Aiton, writing in 1811, it was still a common practice for the herds to light bonfires on the heights to celebrate Beltane (a Celtic festival held on either 1st or 3rd May, and formerly a Quarter Day in Scotland).[128] In particular he cites the fires lit in Ochiltree prior to the May fair and near to Beltane which great numbers of people attended.[129] Similar fires were kindled on the hill at Tarbolton on the evening preceding the fair held on the first Tuesday in June.[130] Here again crowds of people gathered to watch the local youths leaping over the flames. Quite often in the kirk session records, witnesses referred to Beltane when dating particular incidents, so it must have had a significance which distinguished it from other days. At Hallowe'en, traditional rites were performed by single persons eager to determine their fate in the marriage stakes. On that evening, the country folk experienced a mixture of the uncanny sensations associated with proximity to supernatural forces, and innocent fun such as Burns described in his poem "Hallowe'en". Such uncanny feelings provided an exciting contrast to the sober morality imposed by the Kirk.

Even in the houses of the gentry, where formality reigned, gaiety sometimes penetrated the servants' quarters. In the company of David Orr, Burns visited Stair House and entertained the domestic staff with some of his own songs and poems. When Mrs Catherine Stewart of Stair House heard laughter and singing coming from her kitchen, she sent for her housekeeper Mary (Mailly) Crosbie to ascertain the cause of the hilarity, and this led to Burns finding a new friend and patroness.[131]

At Bargany, the eighteenth–century footman, John MacDonald, sometimes assisted the maid to prepare supper in order to allow the first and second cook to go out dancing.[132] Possibly they would attend classes arranged by one of the travelling dancing–masters, or maybe dance penny reels to music played by a local or itinerant fiddler. On the farms when the barley had been harvested and supper of barley–bread, butter, cheese eaten and ale drunk, fiddle music or diddling (singing without words) would provide the music for dancing.[133] This latter celebration was far surpassed by the *kirn* or 'harvest home', which was celebrated in October or November when the harvest was all gathered in. One such, held in the specially decorated granary of Rozelle in November 1840, was attended by a company of 170. The chairman of the festivities was Mr. Walls, the overseer, and the croupier (assistant chairman, whose place was usually at the foot of the table) was Mr. Locke, the gardener. A substantial meal was served, toasts were drunk and dancing continued until an early hour the following morning. The laird's family put in an appearance about eleven o'clock and were greeted by the company.[134] This was probably typical of a *kirn* on any of the local estates.

The flat monumental stones of the local church–yards were used for games such as 'pitch and toss', 'beds' (hopscotch; also known as peevers), and throwing the 'quarter–staff at the gingerbread'. The same location was used by the young men to indulge in 'feats of agility and vigour, in leaping or throwing the hammer or stone.'[135] Cock–fighting was still acceptable in the eighteenth century. In March 1792 James Downie, servant to an innkeeper in Ayr, gave evidence in an assault case which arose from a cock–fight in the Townhead of Ayr.[136]

In May 1857, before she married, Mrs. J. L. Story and her father rented Dankeith House in Symington parish. They engaged a jack–of–all–trades who was supposed to act as coachman and valet and to wait at table and work in the garden, but she discovered that his ample leisure time was chiefly occupied in playing cards with a good–looking parlour maid whom he afterwards married.[137]

During the winter when the ground was too hard to work, curling, 'the roarin' game', was played by all classes of society. In January 1841, players from Old and New Cumnock opposed each other in a match played on the local Bute estate. The match was played at the Woodhead dam, and each side fielded one hundred and sixty players.[138] There can be little doubt that a fair number of the players would be farm servants who, having attended to the animals, would be free to join in the sport, particularly if they were known to be skilled players. Participation in ploughing matches and competition at agricultural shows combined work and pleasure for many male farm workers.

These were opportunities to display their particular skill, possibly to win a prize, to exchange pleasantries with their peers on other farms, and possibly to enjoy a drink. Horseracing too was of interest to all classes of society. In Cumnock, 'The Race' had long been a regular event of the March fair.[139] In Newton–upon–Ayr the local carters raced their horses on the shore and held a parade.[140] In Ayr, too, racing started on the shore before moving to the Old Racecourse.[141] Since the racing there was patronised by the local nobility and gentry[142] and their friends, particularly at the September meeting, many servants would be kept extra busy attending to the horses or catering and cleaning for all who attended the balls and other social functions which took place at that time. In all probability, this would be a time when those servants having direct contact with the society racegoers could expect to receive tips.

In the eighteenth and early nineteenth centuries, a servant's learning to read was very much a matter of chance, and learning to write even more so. John MacDonald recalled that, as a young postilion at Bargany, he had a great desire to learn to read and that the servants gave him a lesson whenever time permitted; also that wherever he went, he took his spelling book with him. It seems that he was fortunate in his employers, for when John Hamilton and Lady Anne became aware of his interest, they arranged that, when they did not require his services, he should attend the local school to be taught reading, writing and arithmetic.[143]

Such an opportunity would probably be less likely for a woman, although in a letter to Alison (or Ellison) Begbie, written at Lochlea in June 1781, Burns referred to her 'charming qualities, heightened by an education much beyond anything I have ever met in any woman I ever dared to approach.'[144] Tradition claims her as a farmer's daughter employed as a domestic servant at Carnell House.[145]

Certainly a senior female servant would be required to have a degree of literacy, examples being the housekeeper at Culzean who kept the account books with their interesting comments,[146] and Miss Craw, the housekeeper at Kirkmichael House, who had responsibility for the children and the house and who corresponded with the agent in the master's absence.[147]

R. A. Houston in his *Scottish Literacy and the Scottish Identity*[148] quoted the case of a girl who taught herself to read, 'by following the minister by my eye on the Bible as he read the portion of Scripture he was going to lecture on.' It seems quite likely that this was not an uncommon practice. In a case of fornication involving Marion MacMillan, servant to John Bell, coachman at Bargany in 1754, she claimed that William Boyle, a servant in Penkill, saw her misconduct with his fellow servant William Crosby through a hole in the door, and told her afterwards 'when he saw her reading her bible.'[149] This testimony endorses John MacDonald's account that the servants at Bargany could read, for Marion MacMillan was not a senior servant to the Hamiltons, but a servant to a servant.

In the kirk session records which I have examined, the female witnesses and some of the men claimed that they could not write. Those men who were able to sign their statement did so with varying levels of proficiency so that in many cases this must have been the limit of their handwriting ability. Even those who had received tuition may have subsequently lost their skill through lack of use. According to William Boyd, 'quite a number of women could read and write', and he cited the claim of Dr. Andrew Edgar, sometime minister of Mauchline, who mentioned, 'the fact of seven witnesses examined and afterwards asked to sign their own depositions in 1764, one was a man who signed his name in almost illegible letters and two of the six women wrote their names in fairly good characters, while three could not write and one could only scratch her initials.'[150]

A servant who worked Culzean signed her name as Jien Aird in November 1752 and as Jean Aird in June 1753. Also at Culzean, in July 1755 James Ross who could provide a full signature was paid exactly the same as James Baird who could barely make his initials, so obviously handwriting was not a requirement for whatever task the Earl employed them to do. Daniel Poison who received £2 10s wages plus £1 6s kitchen money for the year on 5th May 1758 had a very practised handwriting, so one must suppose that his occupation had a need for such a skill.[151]

On 10th November 1770, six male day labourers at Culzean signed for their wages in a fair hand, while John and David Carnochan gave unpractised signatures, and James Baird only his rather crude initials. Of the seven female day labourers, only Janet Limont gave her full signature, Elizabeth Ross no mark at all, and the other five initials not unlike those written by the average modern five–year–old. The same year, of the four gardeners and two day labourers who received pay for work in the garden, the above mentioned James Baird again only provided his crude initials, James McClillan possibly copied his signature, and the other four gave perfectly adequate signatures.[152] By the summer of 1863, Amelia Thomson signed for her own wages and those of two other women, the remaining fifteen other servants each signing in quite fluent hands for their own board and wages. It could be that the two women who did not sign for themselves were otherwise occupied when the payments were being disbursed or that there might still have been servants at Culzean unable to write.[153]

Inability to write did not necessarily mean inability to read, because in the parish schools of the time, fees were charged separately for each of these subjects.

Where servants had learned to read, their texts were probably to be found in the Bible or the Shorter Catechism, and as they became available pleasure would be found in chapbooks. Mr. Tremenheere's Report to the 1867 Royal Commission on Agriculture stated that in Ayrshire the cottars and farm servants had in general received a fair amount of education and that he had not met any 'farm servants or married labourers being unable to read and write, some perhaps imperfectly and awkwardly, but sufficiently well to read a newspaper without difficulty and pen an intelligible letter to their friends.'[154] In keeping with the times in which he lived, Mr. Tremenheere took no evidence from women despite the fact that the report was supposed to be partly about them.

By the time Mrs Hume became the cook at Bargany, she had to write the menu every night on embossed menu cards, and to do this she used both a cookbook and a French dictionary.[155]

In general it must be said, women's education was concerned with domestic skills such as sewing, knitting and housework. Such training was provided in the schools of various types, the poorhouses, the prisons and by 1899, the Glasgow School of Cookery and Domestic Economy was providing a course of six lectures in Ayr Academy on Domestic Economy, at reduced rates for Board School Mistresses. The classes dealt with sanitation, cleaning, servants, food, health and hygiene, and the care of children. According to the *Ayr Advertiser* 'they cannot fail to be in the highest degree interesting and useful to young women of all classes.'[156] Ten years earlier, the same college had provided a series of cookery demonstrations in the Queen's Rooms, Ayr, which were very well attended but, 'comparatively few of the class for whom the lessons were more particularly designed were present.'[157]

Life in a largely rural community has always been conducted in harmony with the natural rhythm of the seasons, so that leisure activities and the acquisition of literacy skills have often been viewed as of secondary importance to the primary tasks of providing food, clothing and shelter. The need to learn to read was promoted by the established church and only later encouraged by the availability of chapbooks, pamphlets, and newspapers before being finally required by the state education system.

[1] *[Old] Statistical Account* Vol. VI, p.55.

[2] *ibid*, p.106.

[3] *ibid*, p.111.

[4] *ibid*, p.480.

[5] *New Statistical Account* Vol. V, p.350.

[6] *ibid*, p.274.

[7] A.A., Kirkoswald Kirk Session Records, CH2/562/1, 7th October 1766.

[8] A.A., Dailly Kirk Session Records, CH2/392/4, 24th September 1808.

[9] Darwin, Tess, *The Scots Herbal,* [Edinburgh, 1996].

[10] *New Statistical Account* Vol. V, p.151.

[11] Darwin, Tess, *The Scots Herbal,* [Edinburgh, 1996], pp. 95–96.

[12] *New Statistical Account* Vol. V, p.653.

[13] *ibid* p.671.

[14] Darwin, Tess, *The Scots Herbal,* [Edinburgh, 1996], p.91.

[15] A.A., Kirkoswald Kirk Session Minutes, CH2/562/2, 28th October 1770.

[16] *[Old] Statistical Account* Vol. VI, p.48.

[17] *[Old] Statistical Account* Vol. VI, p.231.

[18] *ibid*, p.450.

[19] *[Old] Statistical Account* Vol. VI, p.110.

[20] *ibid*, p.480.

[21] *ibid*, p.634.

[22] *ibid*, pp. 529–530.

[23] *New Statistical Account* Vol. V, p.274.

[24] *ibid*, p.310.

[25] Moore, J.M., *An Historical Commemoration of Ayr County Hospital 1888–1991,* [Troon, 1991], pp. 2–3.

[26] Strawhorn, John, *The History of Ayr,* [Edinburgh 1989], p.151.

[27] Moore, J.M., *An Historical Commemoration of Ayr County Hospital 1883–1991,* [Troon, 1991], p.2.

[28] *New Statistical Account* Vol. V, pp. 76–77

[29] Moore, J.M., *An Historical Commemoration of Ayr County Hospital 1883–1991,* [Troon, 1991], pp.1–2.

[30] Kennedy, Jean B., ed., Old Parish Records, Ayr (578) Vol. 9, Deaths, March 1766–May 1820.

[31] A.A., Dailly Kirk Session Records, CH2/392/3,.

[32] Killicoat, Gordon & David, *Tarbolton Churchyard Monumental Inscriptions,* [Ayr, undated], p.9.

[33] Mitchell, Alison, *Pre–1855 Gravestone Inscriptions in Carrick Ayrshire,* [Edinburgh, 1988], p.168.

[34] *ibid*, p.62.

[35] A.A., Ayr Burgh Register of Incarcerations, Liberations, Arrestments and Loosings Thereof, B6/15/7.

[36] *ibid*.

[37] Checkland, S.G., *Scottish Banking, a History, 1695 –1973*, [Glasgow & London], p.130.

[38] *Air Advertiser*, 16th March, 1815.

[39] *ibid*.

[40] *ibid*, 4th May, 1815.

[41] *New Statistical Account* Vol. V, p.78.

[42] *ibid*.

[43] Strawhorn, John, *The History of Ayr, Royal Burgh and County Town*, [Edinburgh, 1989], p.184.

[44] *New Statistical Account* Vol. V, p.79; Pigot's *Directory of Scotland* [1837].

[45] Strawhorn, John, *The History of Ayr, Royal Burgh and County Town*, [Edinburgh, 1989], p.184.

[46] *ibid*, p.211.

[47] *New Statistical Account* Vol. V, p.79.

[48] *ibid*, p.103.

[49] *ibid*, p.167.

[50] *Appendix to the Report on the Poor Laws*, 1844 – Answer to Question 28.

[51] *New Statistical Account* Vol. V, p.79.

[52] *Appendix to the Report on the Poor Laws*, 1844 – Answer to Question 28.

[53] *New Statistical Account* Vol.V, p.391.

[54] *New Statistical Account* Vol. V, p.413.

[55] *Appendix to the Report on the Poor Laws*, 1844 – Answer to Question 28.

[56] *ibid*.

[57] *New Statistical Account* Vol. V, p.625.

[58] *Ayr Advertiser*, 23rd January 1862.

[59] *New Statistical Account* Vol. V, p.490.

[60] *Appendix to the Report on the Poor Laws*, 1844 – Answer to Question 28.

[61] *ibid*.

[62] *New Statistical Account* Vol. V, p.378.

[63] *Appendix to the Report on the Poor Laws*, 1844 – Answer to Question 28.

[64] *New Statistical Account* Vol. V, p.287.

[65] *Appendix to the Report on the Poor Laws*, 1844 – Answer to Question 28.

[66] *New Statistical Account* Vol. V, p.345.

[67] *Appendix to the Report on the Poor Laws*, 1844 – Answer to Question 28.

[68] *New Statistical Account* Vol. V, p.345.

[69] *Appendix to the Report on the Poor Laws*, 1844 – Answer to Question 28.

[70] *New Statistical Account* Vol. V, p.321.

[71] *Appendix to the Report on the Poor Laws*, 1844 – Answer to Question 28.

[72] *ibid*.

[73] *New Statistical Account* Vol. V, p.763.

[74] *Appendix to the Report on the Poor Laws*, 1844 – Answer to Question 28.

[75] Moss, Michael & Slaven, Anthony, *From Ledger Book to Laser Beam*, [Edinburgh, 1992].

[76] *[Old] Statistical Account* Vol. VI Mauchline, p.449.

[77] *ibid.* p.646.

[78] *New Statistical Account* Vol. V, p.80.

[79] *ibid.* p. 157.

[80] *Air Advertiser,* 19th January 1815.

[81] *New Statistical Account* Vol. V, p.124.

[82] *Appendix to the Report on the Poor laws,* 1844 – Answer to Question 28.

[83] *New Statistical Account* Vol. V, p.80.

[84] *Appendix to the Report on the Poor laws,* 1844 – Answer to Question 28.

[85] *New Statistical Account* Vol. V, p.405.

[86] *ibid,* p.377.

[87] *Appendix to the Report on the Poor laws,* 1844 – Answer to Question 28.

[88] West Parish Monthly Letter, Maybole, December 1892.

[89] West Parish Monthly Letter, Maybole, October, 1886.

[90] *ibid.*

[91] Hamilton, Thomas, *Poor Relief in Ayrshire, 1700–1845,* [Edinburgh, 1942], pp. 94–98.

[92] Strawhorn, John, *The New History of Cumnock,* [Cumnock, 1966], p.125.

[93] Campbell, R.H. & Dow, J.B.A., *Source Book of Scottish Economic History,* [Oxford, 1968], pp.178–183.

[94] *ibid.*

[95] A.A., Kyle Union Minute Book 1860–1886, CO3/65/2/1/1.

[96] A.A., Maybole Parochial Board, Register of Applications for Parochial Relief 1855–1865, CO3/50/1/3/7.

[97] A.A., Maybole Combination Poorhouse Board, Minute Book 1865–1876, CO3/50/1/4/1.

[98] A.A., Dailly Kirk Session Records, CH2/392/2.

[99] A.A., Kirkoswald Kirk Session Records, CH2/562/2.

[100] *[Old] Statistical Account* Kirkoswald, p.408.

[101] *ibid.* p.238.

[102] *[Old] Statistical Account* Straiton, p.630/631.

[103] Wilkins, Frances, *Strathclyde's Smuggling Story,* [Kidderminster, 1992], p.58.

[104] *[Old] Statistical Account* Dundonald, p.181.

[105] *[Old] Statistical Account* Ayr, p.43.

[106] Anon, possibly James Paterson, *Reminiscences of Auld Ayr,* [Edinburgh, 1864], pp.77–78.

[107] A.A., Dailly Kirk Session Records, CH2/392/2.

[108] *[Old] Statistical Account* Kirkoswald, p.410.

[109] A.A., Ayr Burgh Register of Incarcerations, Liberations, Arrestments & Loosings Thereof, B6/15/8.

[110] *ibid,* B6/15/7.

[111] A.A., Kirkoswald Kirk Session Minutes, CH2/562/2,.

[112] *ibid.*

[113] A.A., Ayr Burgh Register of Incarcerations, Liberations, Arrestments & Loosings Thereof, B6/15/7.

[114] *ibid,* B6/15/8.

[115] Gray, James T., *Maybole Carrick's Capital,* [Alloway, 1982], p.127.

[116] Strawhorn, John, *The New History of Cumnock,* [Cumnock, 1996], p.64 & p.98.

[117] Warrick, Rev. John, *The History of Old Cumnock,* [Paisley & London, 1899], p.223.

[118] Strawhorn, John, *The History of Prestwick,* [Edinburgh, 1994], p.80.

[119] Hunter, D., Notes compiled for Girvan & District Historical Society.

[120] *ibid.*

[121] Howie, James, *The History of Ayr,* [Kilmarnock, 1861], p.13.

[122] *New Statistical Account* Vol. V, p.83–84.

[123] Criminal Offenders (Scotland), 1846, p.108.

[124] Anon, possibly James Paterson, *Reminiscences of Auld Ayr,* [Edinburgh, 1864], p. 43.

[125] *[Old] Statistical Account* Muirkirk, p.482–483.

[126] *ibid.*

[127] A.A., Maybole Kirk Session Records, CH2/261/1, Dec 3rd 1780.

[128] Aiton, William, *Ayrshire. General view of Agriculture of the County of Ayr* [Glasgow, 1811].

[129] *ibid.*

[130] *[Old] Statistical Account* Tarbolton, p.742.

[131] Boyle, A.M., *The Ayrshire Book of Burns–Lore,* [Alloway, 1985], pp.122–123.

[132] MacDonald, John, *Memoirs of an Eighteenth Century Footman,* [London, 1790], Beresford, John, ed., [London, 1927], p.31.

[133] MacNeill, F. Marion, *The Silver Bough,* Vol.2, [Glasgow, 1959], pp. 125–126.

[134] *Ayr Advertiser,* 26th November 1840.

[135] Mitchell, Rev. John, "Memories of Ayrshire about 1780", in *Miscellany of the Scottish History Society 6* [Edinburgh 1939], pp. 286–288.

[136] Close, Rob, "Cock–fighting in Ayr" in *Ayrshire Notes* No.10, [AANHS, 1996].

[137] Story, J.L., *Early Reminiscences,* [Glasgow, 1911], p.272.

[138] Sanderson, George, *New Cumnock–Far and Away,* [Irvine, 1992].

[139] Warrick, Rev. John, *The History of Old Cumnock,* [Paisley, 1899].

[140] Caldwell, David, *The Kipper Fair,* [Ayr, (1903)], pp.6–11.

[141] Strawhorn, John, *The History of Ayr,* [Edinburgh, 1989], p.129.

[142] *ibid.* p.139.

[143] MacDonald, John, *Memoirs of an Eighteenth Century Footman,* [London, 1790], Beresford, John, ed., [London, 1927], p. 27.

[144] Mackay, J.A., *The Complete Letters of Robert Burns,* [Alloway, 1987], p.47.

[145] *ibid.* p. 43.

[146] N.A.S., Ailsa Muninents, GD 25/9/19,.

[147] A.A., Kennedy of Kirkmichael Papers, ATD60/9/160.

[148] Houston, R.A., *Scottish Literacy and the Scottish Identity,* [Cambridge, 1985], p.136.

[149] A.A., Dailly Kirk Session Records, CH2/392/2, 29th May 1752.

[150] Boyd, William, *Education in Ayrshire Through Seven Centuries,* [London, 1961], p.80.

[151] N.A.S., Ailsa Muniments, GD 25/9/19.

[152] N.A.S., Ailsa Muniments, GD 25/9/14.

[153] N.A.S., Ailsa Muniments, GD 25/9/16.

[154] Report by J.H. Tremenheere, 1867, para. 97.

[155] A.A., Ayrshire Sound Archive, ASA 077, *Life in Domestic Service 1,* 1984.

[156] *Ayr Advertiser,* 2nd February 1899.

[157] *ibid,* 16th January 1889.

Postscript

This monograph concerns a period when servants served individual families rather than a wider public and when people were much more aware of their social position than they are today. It was said that a definition of being middle class was to be able to employ a servant. Regardless of this status symbol aspect of service, the majority of servants fulfilled a very real need economically and the numbers and types of servants employed reflect the activities and economic interest and necessities of the area.

Thus when the estate owners had the leisure and capital to indulge in field sports, some of their servants became gamekeepers as the Servant Tax returns reveal, e.g. from 1785–1787, John Murray was coachman to the Earl of Dumfries, the following year he became coachman and gamekeeper and by 1788–1789 he was classed as gamekeeper.[1]

Likewise, when a gentleman travelled on horseback, he would only have needed to be accompanied by a groom to attend to his horse, but when he travelled by coach, a coachman and one or more postilions would be required not only to attend to the extra horses but to open and close gates and sometimes to help to lift the carriage wheels out of mud and snow. Both positions became redundant to some extent with the arrival of the railway, but certainly with the advent of the car. The implementation of a regular national postal service and later the introduction of the telegraph and telephone services did away with the need for a footman to deliver messages.

Similarly, the availability of piped water and an electricity supply with the possibility of using labour saving devices, helped to reduce the need for resident domestic servants who were replaced by daily help. Instead of giving employment to the washerwoman the commercial laundry or later the domestic washing machine performed her tasks. Today, the hairdresser, the barber and the dry cleaner undertake tasks for the many, previously performed by the valet or the lady's maid for individual employers.

The large houses now have other uses and no longer need a large domestic staff. Culzean is a National Trust property, Auchincruive an agricultural college, Rozelle a local council exhibition centre, and Dumfries House stands empty with an uncertain future.

Cooks and kitchen staff are still employed, but now in hotels and restaurants rather than in private houses. Gardeners too, have changed with the times; there are fewer of them, using power tools and employed either by local authorities or hourly by several householders. Instead of a nanny and nursemaids to care for the children of people of means, there are now nursery nurses and baby sitters to care for the children of the many. The gentry no longer employ governesses to teach their children but send them to school instead. On the farm, the male farm servants became in many cases the skilled ploughmen before they were replaced by tractor men.

The skilled dairymaid and hand milkers have been superseded by the individual milking machine operator and the prized farm cheese has given way to mass–produced cheese from the creameries.

There has been a revolution in service which continues to evolve to cater for the needs and interests of society. Ironically, as new services are being created to cater for the needs of the elderly and the handicapped, an advertisement in the February 1998 issue of *The Scottish Field* magazine, placed by a London based agency, is offering to supply, 'housekeepers, nannies, cooks, butlers, valets, gardeners etc.'[2]

[1] N.A.S., Servant Tax Returns: E 326/5/5, 1785–1786; E 326/5/7, 1786–1787; E 326/5/8, 1787–1788; E 326/5/9, 1788–1789.
[2] *The Scottish Field*, February 1998.

Appendix 1

Kirkdandie Fair

O Robin lad, where hae ye been?
Ye look sae trig and braw, man,
Wi' ruffled sark, and neat and clean,
And Sunday coat and a' man.

Quo' Rab, I had a day to spare,
And I went to Kirkdandie Fair,
Like mony anither gouk to stare,
At a' that could be seen, man.

When climbing o'er the Hadyer Hill,
It wasna han'y wark, man;
And when we cam' to auld Penkill,
We stripped to the sark, man.

The tents, in a' three score and three,
Were planted up and down, man,
While pipes and fiddles thro' the fair,
Gaed bummin' roun' and roun', man.

Here Jamie Brown and Mary Bell,
Were seated on a plank, man,
Wi' Robin Small and Kate Dalziel,
And heartily they drank, man.

And syne upon the board was set,
Gude haggis, though it was na het,
And braxy ham, the landlord cam',
Wi' rowth o' bread and cheese, man.

A country chap had got a drap,
And he gaed thro' the fair, man;
He swore to face wi' twa three chiels,
He wadna muckle care, man.

At length he lent a chiel to clout,
Till his companions turned out,
So on they fell, wi' sic pell–mell,
Till some lay on the ground, man.

O ere the hurry it was o'er,
We scrambled up the brae man,
To try a lass, but she was shy,
A dram she wadna hae, man.

Weel, fare–ye–weel, I carena by,
There's decent lassies here that's dry,
As pretty's you, and no sae shy,
So ony way you like, man.

There's lads and lassies, mony a sort,
Wha cam' for to enjoy the sport;
Perhaps the may be sorry for't,
That ever they cam' there, man.

And mony a lad and lass cam' there,
Sly looks and winks to barter;
And some to fee for hay and hairst,
And others for the quarter.

Some did the thieving trade pursue,
While ithers cam' to sell their woo';
And ithers cam, to weet their mou,
And gang wi' lassies hame, man.

Now, I hae tauld what I hae seen,
I maun be stepping hame, man;
For to be out at twal at e'en,
Would be an unco shame, man.

Besides, my mither said to Kate,
This morning when we took the gate,
Be sure ye dinna stay o'er late,
Come timely hame at e'en, man.

Anon. (Malcolm J. Finlayson, *An Anthology of Carrick,*
[Kilmarnock, 1925.], p. 141.)

Appendix 2: Employment Agencies

Date	Name	Address
1849–50	Mrs. Sprent	Kirk Port, High Street.
1858–65	Sprent / Mrs. Baird	6 Kirk Port, High Street
1867–71	Mrs. Baird	Kirk Port, High Street
1873–81	Mrs. Baird	8 Kirk Port, High Street
1882–83	Mrs. Baird	7 Kirk Port, High Street
1861–62	Mrs. Corner	32 Sandgate (Wm. Corner, Perfumer & Hairdresser)
1864–71	Mrs. Corner	20 Sandgate
1873–74	Wm. Corner	20 Sandgate
1864–68	Mrs. James Cowan	2 Sandgate Street
1886–95	Mrs. Cowan	82 Sandgate Street
1861	Peter McConnell	234 High Street
1864 –77	Peter McConnell	235 High Street
1878–79	John McConnell	36 Alloway Street
1880–81	John McConnell	233 High Street
1882–83	John McConnell	237 High Street
1884–85	John McConnell	241 High Street
1886–87	John McConnell	233 High Street
1864–65	Miss Jane Wilson	68 Sandgate St. (Fruiterers & Reg. Office).
1870–71	Miss Murdoch	8 Fort Street (Mangle Keeper & Register for Servants)
1873–79	Miss Murdoch	15 Cathcart Street
1880–81	Miss Murdoch	25 New Road
1882–83	Miss Murdoch	49 New Road
1873–74	Mrs. W. Black	250 $^{1}/_{2}$ High Street
1909–10	Alex. Redpath	79 Dalblair Road
1873–81	Wm. C. Currie	62 Sandgate Street
1882–85	Wm. C. Currie	76 Sandgate Street
1886–90	Mrs. Currie	80 Sandgate Street
1873–81	Mrs. Gribbon	32 Alloway Street
1882–87	Mrs. Gribbon	49 Alloway Street
1889–90	Mrs. Gribbon	18 Mill Street
1873–74	Hugh Brown	40 ½ Sandgate Street
1873–81	Miss E. Hunter	152 High Street
1889–95	Mrs. James Clark	80 Sandgate Street
1896–99	Mrs. James Clark	82 Sandgate Street (Coal Merchant & Agent for Steamers).
1894–95	Miss Loudon	4 B New Bridge Street
1898–99	Miss Orr	17 Alloway Street
1896–99	W. A. Langton	47 Sandgate Street
1900–01	Mrs. W. A. Langton	51 Sandgate Street
1902–11	Mrs. W. A. Langton	63 Sandgate Street
1896–99	James Scott	6 New Bridge Street

1900–05	James Scott	68 Newmarket Street
1906–12	Scott's Registry	68 Newmarket Street
1912–15	Scott's Registry	36 Newmarket Street
1898–1908	James Fraser	63 Alloway Street
1908–10	Fraser, B. B.	63 Alloway Street
1876–77	Mrs. Whitelaw	8 Fort Street
1880–87	Mrs. T. Jack	5 Newmarket Street
1889–90	Mrs. T. Jack	67 Newmarket Street & 216 High Street
1890–91	Mrs. T. Jack	67 & 69 Newmarket Street & 197 High Street
1891–95	Mrs. T. Jack	67 & 69 Newmarket Street
1880–83	Mrs. Thomas Lambie	4 New Bridge Street
1884–85	Mrs. T. Lambie	6 New Bridge Street
1886–87	Mrs. T. Lambie	6A New Bridge Street
1889–91	Mrs. T. Lambie	4 New Bridge Street
1882–85	Wm. Hall	84 Sandgate Street
1900–09	Mrs. Cameron	84 Sandgate Street
1900–01	Miss. J. Goudie	73 Alloway Street
1902–07	Mrs J. Goudie	43 Kyle Street
1907–14	Goudie's Registry	43 Kyle Street
1914–15	Goudie's Registry	55 Kyle Street
1900–01	Hugh Henry	35 Newmarket Street
1900–15	Mrs. Hess	7 Killoch Place, Beresford Terrace
1900–01	Mrs. D. C. Spencer	82 Sandgate, (Coal, Greenan Steam Laundry)
1906–12	Hugh Murray	4B New Bridge Street
1902–05	Hunters	4 Sandgate
1906–15	Hunters	21 Sandgate
1902–05	John V. Thomson	79 Dalblair Road
1906–15	John V. Thomson	4 Old Bridge Street
1903–15	Miss Jones	45 Carrick Street
1906–07	Country Registry	28 Smith Street
1907–09	Country Registry	61 Kyle Street
1909–10	Country Registry	57 Kyle Street
1910–11	Country Registry	67 Kyle Street
1906–09	Joseph W. Provan	87 South Harbour Street
1889–90	Miss Miller	39 Alloway Street
1889–93	Mrs McWhinnie	224 High Street
1882–83	Daniel McKechnie	152 High Street
1884–87	D. McKechnie	224 High Street
1882–95	Miss Paul	43 Carrick Street
1896–1903	Miss Paul	45 Carrick Street
1886–90	George Arbuckle	8 River Street

Compiled from: Lockhart, Charles *Directory for Ayr, Newton, Wallacetown, St. Quivox, Prestwick and Newton.* 1845–46, Ayr Observer Office; Post Office *Directory for Ayr, Newton and Wallacetown,* 1849–50–1870–71, Ayr Observer Office; Post Office *General and Trades Directory for Ayr, Newton and Wallacetown,* 1873–74 to 1914–15.

Appendix 3

Rules and Regulations

Of the Female Friendly Society for the Town and Parish of Ayr
Instituted Decr 1st, 1804

Introduction

As nothing tends more to the happiness of Society than the discovery and application of practical methods of alleviating the misery and increasing the comforts of our fellow Creatures, more especially those who are descending into the vale of life, and who by the course of nature are not likely to be long in a Condition to support themselves, so to the honour of our Country it may be justly said, no nation has done more to carry these methods into effect, witness the numberless Friendly societies established in every quarter for the benefit and support of their Members of which more than one exists among ourselves.

To the Credit of some benevolent Ladies in this place one of these Societies has lately been instituted here, and patronized by them, it has given relief to a number of the indigent of their own sex and has been conducted upon such principles, and by such Rules, as at this moment to be in a very flourishing Condition, and from the very great success they have had in that laudable Institution, the present Scheme is proposed with a view to follow out their benevolent plan by beginning at the Class of Females where the Ayr Female Friendly Society left off viz. At the age of *Forty.*

Article 1st

The purpose of the Society is, to raise a fund by admission Money, by a regular Contribution from its Members, and by voluntary Donations from all who wish well to the plan for the relief of its *general* members when rendered unable to work by Sickness, Infirmity, or old age. It shall be called *The Female Friendly Society* for the *Town and Parish of Air.*

Article II

The Society shall consist of two Classes viz. the class of *Honorary* Members, who besides their contributions, may be willing to dedicate a portion of their time to the Management of the Society's affairs, and who are not to be limited to any Number, or restricted to any age, and the Class of *General* members, for whose advantage *alone* this Institution is formed, and who are never to exceed *Forty five.*

Article III

Every person proposing to become a general member shall be admitted or rejected, by a majority of votes; she must be above the age of *Forty,* and not exceeding *Sixty five* years, of healthy constitution, good Character, able to earn a livelihood, and manage the affairs of a family, born, or long residing in the town or Parish of Ayr.

Article IV

Each honorary member when admitted into the Society shall pay at least *Five Shillings,* and a yearly contribution of *Four shillings and four pence* in quarterly payments of *Thirteen pence,* beginning the first quarter payment on or before the first quarterly Meeting of the Committee, after her admission. An honorary Member shall have it in her power to pass into the class of general Members, if she has been five years in the Society, and was under Sixty five years when she entered it. Each *General* Member shall pay of entry Money, *Two shillings and sixpence,* and a quarterly contribution of *Thirteen pence* in the same manner as the honorary members. An honorary member to pay sixpence for a Copy of these Rules, and a General Member Threepence.

Every Member at her admission shall receive a printed Ticket, signed by the Secretary, bearing her Name and date of being admitted.

If any General Member residing in Ayr, or the Parish, shall neglect to pay her quarterly Contribution, regularly, she shall incur, for the arrear of the first quarter Two pence, for the second Four Pence, for the third Six pence; and if the arrears and fines are not paid on the fourth quarter day she shall forfeit all right to the privileges of the Society.

If any general Member shall not continue to reside within Ayr or the Parish and shall fail to remit her quarterly contribution fee of all expense, she shall, for two quarters arrears be liable in a fine of Two pence for three quarters, Fourpence, for the four quarters sixpence and for five on the sixth Quarter Day, she shall forfeit all right to privileges of the Society. No persons owing quarterly assessments or fines can vote either in the Committee or at the General Meeting.

Article V

The Society shall hold their first General Meeting of the Second Monday of January 1805 in the Academy Hall and shall continue to meet every year on the second Monday of January at the same hour viz. one o clock.

At the first Meeting as above, and annually thereafter, the Society shall first proceed to choose a President, then a Vice President, a Treasurer & Secretary. These four with eight other Members to be chosen at the same Meeting (five from the honorary, and three from the general members) shall form a Committee to conduct the affairs of the Society. This Committee (five of whom to be a quorum) shall statedly meet four times in the year viz. On the first Monday of March, of June, of September, and of December, and also at other times when necessary to manage the Funds, give supplies to those whose situation may require them, impose reasonable Fines, and decide in any Bussiness which relates to the Society.

To the Committee shall be given, on the first Monday of December at the latest, the names of those who are to be proposed as general members, and if the Circumstances mentioned in the 3d Article be not known to the Members of the Committee, an attestation of them by a Surgeon and Minister, or two Elders, will be required and must be lodged with the President, or Secretary, ten days at least before the General Meeting at which the person is to be proposed.

If any Member impose on the Society, in any of the particulars mentioned in the said 3d Article, and if it be proved within one year from the date of her admission, she shall be instantly expelled the Society, and forfeit any sums of money she may have paid.

All new Regulations or alterations of those which may have been in use, shall be proposed to the Committee and by them rejected or laid before the General Annual Meeting, and the General Meeting by a Majority of votes, may make additions to the Rules of the Society, or alterations of them as they see proper, provided always these are not repugnant to the laws of the Realm, or to the Act of Parliament passed in the thirty third year of the reign of his present Majesty, for the encouragement and Relief of Friendly Societies.

The Committee shall keep regular Minutes of their Proceedings, which shall be read at the annual general Meeting who retain the power of altering any of the Committee's decisions.

At the general Meeting, when the Office Bearers of the Society, and other Members of the Committee, are to be chosen, those of the proceeding year may be re–elected, but if any change is to be made, four members at least, of the old Committee must be continued.

The president, with the concurrence of a Majority of the Committee, may at any time call an extraordinary Meeting of the Society giving the whole Members due previous notice thereof.

The Society shall also, at the annual Meeting, elect an Officer, who shall at the desire of the president, summon the Members of the Committee & of the whole Society to their respective meetings, and collect from the Members their quarterly contributions, on the Monday before the Meeting of the Committee, and pay the same to the Treasurer, giving her at the same time a distinct account of those in arrears.   For which trouble each Member upon the fourth quarter day, shall be obliged to pay the Officer *Twopence.* If no member will officiate in this capacity, any other person willing may be chosen.

The Members, when assembled, shall behave respectfully to one another; no Conversation shall be permitted to take place at any of the Meetings of the Society, nor any question or debate, except what immediately relates to the business before the Meeting under pain of expulsion, And when members speak on any subject under discussion, they must always address the President.

All fines imposed by these Rules, or to be imposed by the Committee, shall be paid to the Treasurer, and make part of the Funds of the Society.

Article VI

When any member shall be confined to bed, by Sickness, Accident, or bodily Infirmity; and wholly disabled from working, she shall make known her case to the Committee, who will order her so much weekly, as her situation and state of the funds will admit. And when the member is not wholly disabled, but may contribute something to her own support by making Application to the Committee, she shall receive a modified allowance at their discretion. But in neither case is supply to be given unless all quarterly assessments due to the Society are paid up.

At the death of any General Member, the Committee shall order the Treasurer to pay Half a Guinea towards defraying funeral expenses if required. Every Member, receiving aid on account of Indisposition, shall, nevertheless, continue to pay her quarterly and other contributions, and shall when recovered give immediate intimation to the Secretary, or, if residing at a distance shall send notice of her recovery, in order that all further payments may be stopped; and if any member be guilty of fraud, by receiving her allowance after her recovery, she shall forfeit all right to the privileges of the Society.

Article VII

Every Member, who after her admission shall leave the parish of Air, and who shall need the aid of this fund, must send a Certificate to the President, attested by a Surgeon and the Minister of the Parish where she resides, and mention the mode of conveying the Supply; which shall be sent, after deduction any Assessments and fines that she may be owing.

Article VIII

The President shall appoint two of the Committee, by rotation each quarter as visitors who by themselves or proper Deputies shall go every week to any Member getting support, and may take a Surgeon with them, and give in a Report to the President, who shall regularly send by these Visitors, or the Officer the weekly allowance, to which she shall be entitled.　Should any complaining member refused to be examined, or to follow the prescription of a Surgeon, she shall be excluded the Society, and deemed an Impostor or should any Visitor, when ordered by the President, to visit any deceased Member neglect to return a report within twenty four hours, unless she can assign a sufficient excuse, she shall forfeit Two shillings and sixpence.

Article IX

If any member shall be convicted of a criminal offence before any Court she shall be expelled the Society for two years at the end of which period if she shall bring proof to the Society of her repentance and good conduct, she shall be admitted paying her arrears.

Article X

Three weeks before every general Meeting in January, the Treasurer shall lodge her accounts with the Secretary, and the Committee shall name either one of their own number, or some other person having knowledge in accounts, to examine the same, and report to the Committee who shall lay them before the General Meeting with their option thereon, and by the Society they shall be finally adjusted.

Article XI

All sums of money received by the Treasurer, on account of the Society shall be lodged in the hands of Messrs Hunters & Co Bankers in Ayr in name of the President or her successor in office for behalf of the Society there to remain until otherwise disposed of to the best advantage as a majority of the subscribers shall determine.

Article XII

A list of all persons in arrears, shall be publicly read at the second meeting of the Committee next after the days of payment, and at all other Meetings as well ordinary as extraordinary; such list shall be laid upon the Table for the perusal of the Members present.

Article XIII

In case of any dispute arising in the Society, it shall be stated to the President, who shall see the same settled by a Majority of votes.

Article XIV

This Society shall not be dissolved, or the funds divided, but by unanimous consent of the existing Members thereof, unless the funds shall be inadequate to the support of its Members; in that case as in others a Majority may dissolve the Society

Therefore we the subscribers Bind and Oblige ourselves to abide by the foregoing Rules and Regulations in every respect.

At Ayr the twenty ninth day of October One thousand eight hundred and five years. The day in which His Majesty's Justices of Peace for the County of Ayr met at their General Quarter Sessions Having Considered the foregoing Rules and Regulations They Approved thereof and Gave their Sanction thereto agreeable to Act of Parliament.

Sanctioned 29th Octr 1805

Appendix 4: Tables of Wages and Prices

The tables of wages and prices below have been compiled from the *Statistical Account of Scotland* 1791–1799, the *New Statistical Account of Scotland* 1837–1841 and the "Report of the Royal Commission on the Poor Laws in Scotland, Appendix Part IV", 1844.

Table of Wages

Parish	Year	Servants		Day Labourers		
		Male	**Female**	**Men**	**Women**	**Children > 9 yrs**
Auchinleck	1752	£4–£7	£1 13s 4d	8d		
	1791–2	£8–£9	£5	1s		
	1844	£22 without board		9s–10s a week	sometimes 1s–1s 3d; usually higher during harvest	
Ayr	1790			7s a week or a little more		
	1837	£12 with bed and board	£6 with bed and board	8s weekly in winter; 9s weekly in summer; 2s 6d a day in harvest		
	1844	£14 with bed and board		1s 6d a day	9d a day	
Ballantrae	1790	£6–£7 £10 with cottagers benefit				
	1837	£19–£23 with cottage and unspecified benefits	£2–£4 half yearly. £5 half yearly for experienced dairy maids	1s–1s 4d in winter. 1s 6d–1s 8d in summer; or 1s 4d winter and summer	8d a day for field workers	
	1844			6s–9s a week		
Barr	earlier than 1844			6s–9s a week		
	1844	£10 with bed and board		1s 10d	10d a day	

Parish	Year	Servants		Day Labourers		
		Male	Female	Men	Women	Children > 9 yrs
Colmonell	1838	£12–£14	£5–£6	1s 4d–1s 6d a day without victuals	9d a day	
	1844	£12 a year		9s a week	4s a week	
Coylton	1790			1s a day		
	1791	£14 a year	£3 a year			
	1844	£13 with bed and board	£6 a year with bed, board and washing	9s a week; young people 10da day in harvest	10d a day; 1s 6d a day in harvest	4d–6d according to age
Craigie	1790–1	£9–£10	£3–£4	1s in winter; 1s 3d in summer; 1s 5d– 1s 10d in harvest		
	1844	£24 a year		1s 8d a day	10d–1s	
New Cumnock	1837			10s a week		
	1844	£14		1s 8d a day	10d a day	6d a day
Old Cumnock	1792	£7 10s	£2–£4	10d–15d a day without meat; 25s for harvest	18s for harvest	
	1837	£10–£14	£3–£4 a half year for dairy maids	1s 6d–1s 8d a day		
	1844	£8–£14		1s 4d–1s 8d	very seldom employed in fields	
Dailly	1730s	£1 a year	13s 4d plus an apron and a pair of shoes	2d a day with victuals		
	1792	£6–£9 a year	£2 10s–£4	8d–10d in 4 winter months; 10d–1s in summer; much more in harvest		
	1844	£11		1s 6d a day	7d	6d
Dalmellington	1844	£12 a year		1s 6d a day		
Dalrymple	1790–91	£3–£3 10s a year for married men		10d–1s 5d a day		

Parish	Year	Servants		Day Labourers		
		Male	Female	Men	Women	Children > 9 yrs
Dalrymple (cont.)	1837	£10–£16 with free house, garden; 2 pecks meal, 2 pecks potatoes & 1 cwt. coal a week		1s–1s 6d with victuals. 1s 6d–2s without victuals		
	1844	£20–£36 in both cash and kind		20d a day	8d–1s 6d a day	
Dundonald	1844	£8 a year with bed, board and washing		1s 10d a day	occasionally 1s a day	4d–6d according to ability
Galston	1844			1s 6d–1s 8d on average		
Girvan	1817– 1822 approx.	£20 with bed and board				
	1837	£14–£16 with bed and board; lads, able for most work, £9– £12	dairy maids, £8. Town housemaids, £4–£7	1s 6d a day without victuals for shearers		
	1844	£14 with bed and board		1s 6d a day	8d a day	
Kirkmichael	1792	£7 with bed and board and washing; £4–£6 with house & yard, fuel, 6½ bolls of meal, ground to grow potatoes, grass & fodder for his cow – £13– £15 in all	£3 with bed, board and washing	8d–1s in winter; 10d– 15d in summer		
	1844	£20 without victuals			4d–9d a day; very few work in fields	

Parish	Year	Servants		Day Labourers		
		Male	Female	Men	Women	Children > 9 yrs
Kirkoswald	1792	£6 with bed and board; £5, married men, with house, yard, 6½ bolls of meal, ground for potatoes; to have a milch cow maintained summer and winter	£3 with bed and board			
	1844	£25		1s–1s 8d a day	8d a day	
Mauchline	1844	£7 10s. a half year		1s 8d 2s in harvest	1s 6d a day seed time and harvest	
Maybole	1844	£12–£14 with board and lodging; £12–£14, married men, with house and garden; 6½ bolls of meal, 6½ bolls of potatoes		1s 6d a day	6d–8d a day	food and clothing for boys herding cattle
Monkton and Prestwick	1791–93	£8–£10	£3 10s–£4	10d in winter (Martinmas–New Year's Day); 1s in summer; 14d–16d in harvest		
	1844	£14 with house, garden, potatoes to value of £8 6s 6d, with coal driven free		9s–10s a week	10d–1s a day spring and summer; 1s 6d–2s in harvest	6d–8d a day

Parish	Year	Servants		Day Labourers		
		Male	Female	Men	Women	Children > 9 yrs
Muirkirk	1792–93	£8–£12 a year with victuals	£3–£4	1s 2d–1s 6d a day with victuals; 1s 3d a day with victuals for mowers		
	1844	£20–£26 a year including allowances		1s 4d–1s 6d a day	10d a day	6d–8d a day
Newton upon Ayr	1844			1s 8d a day	8d–1s a day	
Ochiltree	1837	£12 10s	£7 with lodging, food and washing	1s 3d in winter; 1s 8d in summer		
	1844	£13, ploughmen; £8, young lads		1s 6d a day	not usually employed	
Riccarton	1792	£6–£9 a year	£3–£4	1s in winter, 14d in summer; without their meat		
	1839	£12–£16 with food	£7–£10	10s in winter; 12s in summer		
	1844	£12–£18		2s–4s a day; not employed every day.	occasionally employed; 9d–1s a day.	
Straiton	1837	£13 a year for a ploughman living in master's house; shepherds chiefly paid by certain privileges believed to secure them more comfort than a labourer	£7 10s for a good servant, for whom there is more than usual demand			4s in summer in turnip fields

Parish	Year	Servants		Day Labourers		
		Male	**Female**	**Men**	**Women**	**Children > 9 yrs**
Straiton (cont.)	1844	£12 with bed and board. £12 with house and garden; 6½ bolls of meal and 6 bolls of potatoes		9s a week	9d a day in summer	
Symington	1792	£8–£9, able to "plow"	£3–£4 a year			
	1844	2s a day		9s a week	8d–10d a day	
Tarbolton	1844			1s 8d a day		

Table of Prices

Parish	Year	Meal	Potatoes	Coal
Auchinleck	1844	16s	9s a boll	4d a cwt.
Ayr	1790	16s–18s a boll (oats)		2s 3d–2s 4d a cart at the pit
		a day labourer with a wife and 5 children could purchase in a year on average: 3 pecks of meal, a greater quantity of potatoes, half a cart of coal, soap worth 2d, 3 stone of wool at 7s 6d the stone for clothing and 10lbs. of lint at 10d a lb.		
	1791			2s a cart (8s a ton)
	1844	18s 6d a boll (140lbs.)	10s 6d a boll (608lbs.)	7s 10d a ton
Ballantrae	1836	2s 3d a stone (retail)		peat abundant; coals 10s 10d a cart (5 creels).
	1844	17s 5½d for 140lbs.		
Colmonell	1844	15s 6d a boll	6s 6d a boll	15s a ton
Coylton	1844	17s 0½d a boll wholesale	10d a boll	2¾d a cwt. or 6s a ton at pits
Craigie	1844	15s a boll	8s a boll	5s a ton at pits
New Cumnock	1844	35s a load	10s a boll	2s 6d a cart of 12cwt.
Old Cumnock	1792	11d–11½d a peck		2s 2d a cart of 9cwt.[1]
	1844	1s 11½d an imperial stone	10s 6d an Ayrshire boll	9d a load
Dailly	1792	16s a boll	8s a stone	3s 4d a ton
	1844	15s an imperial boll	8s a boll	7d a creel of 3cwt.
Dalmellington	1837			3s. 6d. an imperial ton
	1844	15s a boll	8s a boll	3s a ton plus carting and toll 1s
Dalrymple	1790–91			4d–6d a load (coal or peat)
	1837			13s a ton including carriage
	1844	15s 6d a boll	8s a boll	13s 6d a ton
Dundonald	1792			8d–10d a cart load
	1841			1s a load of 4cwt.
	1844	17s 5d a boll	8d a peck	3d a cwt. at pits
Galston	1837			4s a ton plus carriage
Girvan	1844	13s 6d a boll	7s a boll	9s 6d a ton
Kirkmichael	1838			4s 7½d a cart of 12cwt. (5 creels)
Kirkoswald	1844	280 imperial lbs.: oatmeal 32s; wheat 57s	32s a ton	
Mauchline	1844	1s a peck	10s a boll	6s a cart of 14cwt.
Maybole	1837			7s 6d–10s a ton
Monkton and Prestwick	1837			5s–5s 9d a horse cart load
	1844	17s 3d a boll (140lbs.)	2s 6d a cwt.	8s a ton plus 1s 6d cartage
Muirkirk	1792–93	16s–17s 4d a boll		
	1844	20s a boll (140lbs.)	12s 6d a boll	2s 6d a cart of 14cwt.

Parish	Year	Meal	Potatoes	Coal
Newton– upon–Ayr	1791			5s 6d a tun (24cwt.)
	1837			6s 9d a cart load
	1844			10s–10s 6d a ton; now 11s
Ochiltree	1844	Prices fixed by fiars		
Riccarton	1839			5s–6s an imperial ton
	1844	16s a boll	13s	5s 6d a ton at pit
St. Quivox	1844	15s a boll	10s an Ayrshire boll	7s 6d–9s a ton at pit
Som	1837			5s 3d a cart (12cwt.)
	1844	16s a boll	8s a boll	6s–8s a ton
Stair	1844			
Straiton	1837			8s an imperial ton; 3s 6d in Patna
	1844	17s 6d a boll	8s a boll	
Symington	1844	28s a load	32s a load	3s for six loads (1 ton)
Tarbolton	1842			6s a ton
	1844	nothing peculiar		

[1] Appears as "900cwt." in the original.

Appendix 5: Servant Tax Returns

Abstracted from Servant Tax records for 5th April 1787 to 5th April 1788: E326/5/9 (male) and E326/6/9 (female).

Note: * "a Bachelor"

Parish	Master & Mistress Names & Designations	Servants' Names	Quality
	Male Servants		
St. Quivox	Richard Campbell Esq.	David Shaw	H. Servant
	William Campbell Esq.	Gabriel Armour	H. Servant
	Craigie*	Hugh Hunter	Coachman
		William Merchant	Gardener
	Mr Oswald Auchincruive	Thomas Lowden	Gardener
	at Auchincruive	James Taylor	H. Servant
	at London	Thomas Daniel	Butler
Monkton	James Dalrymple Esq.	James Guthrie	Gardener
		Allan Wallace	H. S.
	Robert Reid Esq.	Daniel Baird	H. Servant
	Mr Mitchell, Minister	James McCraik	Postilion
Dundonald	Moses Crawford Esq.	Andrew Neilson	Postilion
		Lewis De Creux	H. Servant
	Mrs Fullarton of Fullarton	John McKie	H. Servant
		Chas. Anderson	Gardener
		Willm. Clairchue	Postilion
	Mr McKerrell of Hillhouse	James Gowdie	Postilion
		James Smith	Footman
	Alexr. Fairlie of Fairlie Esq.*	Nathaniel Wilson	Butler
		William Lennox	Coachman
		John Allan	Footman
	Sir Wm. Cunningham at Holms*	James Garret	Gardner
		Alexr. Dunlop	Groom
Symington	Capt. Kelso of Dankeith	David Logan	Postilion
		Thomas Andrew	House Servant
	William Fullarton Esq. Rosemount	Thomas Laidley	Postilion & Gamekeeper
		John Bruce	Gardner
		James McGregor	H. Servt. & Gamekeeper
Tarbolton	Col. Montgomery Coilsfield	James McPherson	H. S.
		unnamed	cook
		Hugh Paterson	Postilion
		James McClelland	Gardener
	Mr Cunningham Annbank	Chas. Robinson	H. S.
		Robert Dick	Groom
Craigie	Capt. Wm. Cairnhill*	John Tafferd	H. S.
Mauchline	Claud Alexander Esq.*	John Livingston	Gardener

Parish	Master & Mistress Names & Designations	Servants' Names	Quality
		George Fleming	Liveryman
		David Brown	Liveryman
		James King	Liveryman
		Thomas Robb	Liveryman
		Peter Kerr	Liveryman
Sorn	John F. Gray Esq.	James Milliken	H. S.
	Professor Stewart	William Mill	H. S.
	Neil Campbell Esq. Sorn Castle	George Bowrie	Gardener
		James Baird	H. S.
	James Tennant Esq.*	Thomas Sanders	H. S.
Dalrymple	Hugh Ross Esq. of Kerse*	John M. Clannachan	Gardener
		John McKelvie	H. Servant
Kirkmichael	James Whitefoord Esq.*	Andrew Haikston	Gardener
	David Kennedy Esq.*	unnamed	Gardener
Maybole	Thomas Kennedy Esq. Greenan	James Johnston	Gardener
		Duncan Kennedy	Groom
		Joseph West	Footman
		John McCreadie	Gamekeeper
	William Crawford Esq. Doonside	John Craig	Footman
		John Cowan	Gardener
	Miss Hutchison Monkwood	Thomas McHarg	Chaise Driver
	Col. Hunter Newark*	Archd. Menzies	Footman
		Thomas McColm	Postilion
		Robert Kennedy	Gardener
	John McMicken Esq.	unnamed	H. S.
Kirkoswald	Earl of Cassillis*	Mawle Thomson	Gardener
		David Walker	Gardener
		Gilbert McHaffie	Butler & Valet
		John Hunter	Cook
		Alexander Douglas	Footman
		James Anderson	?
		John Wolf	Coachman
		William Mellvill	Postilion
		Hugh Mann	Porter
		John Cuthbert	Groom
		Thomas Rewcastle	Gamekeeper
Dailly	Sir Andrew Cathcart of Carleton*	Hugh Guthrie	H.S.
		unnamed	Postilion
	Sir Adam Fergusson of Kilkerran*	Alexander Grant	Gardener
		Robert McMillan	Groom
		Duncan Watt	Coachman
		James McClure	H. Servant
		William Rewcastle	Gamekeeper
	John Hamilton of Bargany	George Ainsley	Butler
		Andrew Jackson	Valet

Parish	Master & Mistress Names & Designations	Servants' Names	Quality
		David Crawford	Gardener
		George Stewart	Footman
		John Jackson	Coachman
		Adam Hendry	Postilion
	Capt. Kennedy Drummellan	William Riggs	H. Servant
Straiton	John McAdam Esq.	James Ritchison	Gardener
	Craigengillan	Thomas McPherson	H. S. & G. K.
		Gibt. McKinlay	Chaise Driver
	Quintin McAdam Esq.	James Clark	a deputation?
Barr	David Kennedy Martin Esq. Bellimore*	Humphry Pennycuik	H. S.
Old Cumnock	Earl of Dumfries	Gilbert Ross	Gardener
		John Murray	Coachman & gamekeeper
		Wm. Bannatyne	Porter & Gamekeeper
	Hugh Logan of Logan Esq.*	Archd. Baird	H. S. & Gamekeeper
Auchinleck	James Boswell Esq.	Robert Paton	Gardener
		James Ross	Footman
Ochiltree	Adam Crawford Newall Esq.	David Rowan	Postilion
	Polquhairn	John Drummond	Gardener
Coylton	John Steele Esq. Gadgirth	Thomas Andrew	H. S. & Postilion
	James Hamilton Esq. Sundrum	Charles Shaw	H. S.
		William Forrester	Gardener
		Hugh McCreath	Postilion
Stair	Mungo Smith Esq. Drongan	Quintin Morton	H. S. & Postilion
		James Duff	Gardener
	Lord Justice Clerk at Barskimming	James McKerran	Gamekeeper
	General Stewart at Stair	William Campbell	Gardener

Parish	Master & Mistress Names & Designations	Servants' Names	Quality
		Female Servants	
St. Quivox	Mr Murray Excise Officer	Janet McConchie	
	Mr Taylor Seceding Minister	Betty Hunter	
	W. Neil Mount Hamilton	Agnes Borland	
	Richd. Campbell Esq.	Jean Mitchell	
	Wm. Campbell Esq. of	Jean Thomson	C. Maid
	Craigie*	Mary Watt	Cook
	Mr Oswald at Auchincruive	Jean Shaw	H. keeper
		Margt. Watt	C. Maid

Parish	Master & Mistress Names & Designations	Servants' Names	Quality
	at London	Mary Bowes	H. K. & Cook
		Margt. Angele	H. Maid
		Sarah Silvie	C. Maid
		Mary Taylor	K. Maid
Monkton	Mr Tarbet of the Austens	Janet McNeillie	
	Major Macdonald	Janet Withers	
	Capt. Hathorn*	Margt. Dock	
	James Dalrymple Esq.	Mrs Kennedy	
		Margt. Woodburn	
	Robt. Reid Esq. Adamton	Nancy Brown	
	James Rorrison Esq. Ladykirk	Elizth. Dow	
	Wm. Mitchell Minister*	Margt. Dick	
Dundonald	Crawford Esq. Newfield	Martha McLachlan	
		Nelly Fraser	
	Mr Fullarton of Fullarton	Mrs Anderson	
		Alison Sheills	
		Mary Cunningham	
		Barbara Fullarton	
	Mr McKerrell, Hillhouse	Janet Hunter	
	Alex. Fairlie of Fairlie Esq.*	Mrs McWhirter	
		Ann Jamieson	
		Nancy McDowall	
	Sir William Cunningham at Holms*	Ann Ronaldson	
		Margt. McFie	
	Mr Duncan Minister	Jean Wyllie	
Symington	William Boyd Townend*	Jean Wallace	
	Capt. Kelso of Dankeith	Isobel Cameron	
		Margt. Houston	
	William Fullarton of Rosemount Esq.	Elizabeth Bllellock?	
		Isobel Kerr	
		Helen Rodger	
		Jean Eagleson	
	Mr Logan Minister	Agnes McJanet	
Tarbolton	Col. Montgomery Coilsfield	Isobel Campbell	
		Janet Hunter	
	Wm. Cunningham of Annbank Esq.*	Janet Dunlop	
	James Manson Innkeeper	Janet Drennan	
	Mr Woodrow Minister	Mary McKie	
Craigie	Capt. Wallace of Cairnhill*	unnamed	
Mauchline	Miss Campbells Mauchline	Elizabeth Richmond	
	Miss Wallace	Elizabeth Campbell	
	Mrs Campbell Netherplace	Agnes Paterson	
	James Lammie mercht.	Janet Patrick	

Parish	Master & Mistress Names & Designations	Servants' Names	Quality
	Mr McGill Kingencleuch	unnamed	
	Claud Alexander of Ballochmyle Esq.*	Janet Farquhar Ann Finlay Beanie Brown	
	Mr Rounald Tobacconist*	Agnes Broadfoot	
Sorn	John Farquhar Gray Esq. Gilmilnscroft	Janet Drennan	
	Professor Stewart	Elizth. Watt Rebecca Johnston	
	Neil Campbell Esq. Sorn Castle	Lilias Turner	
Dalrymple	Hugh Ross Esq. of Kerse*	Mary Campbell Jean Hutchison	
Kirkmichael	James Whitefoord Esq. of Dunduff a Minor	Ann Edgar	
	Mr Ramsay Minister	unnamed	
	Allan Bell in Garfar	Marion Eaglesom	
Kirkoswald	Earl of Cassillis*	Agnes Arthur Jean Kennedy Rachael Kelly	
	Mr Biggar Minister	Elizabeth Underwood	
Girvan	Doctor McIntyre	Isobel Sillars	
	Capt. Downie Girvan	Mary McLeod	
	Mr Thomson Minister	Janet Alexander	
Maybole	Thos. Kennedy Esq. Greenan	Sarah Donald Agnes Gray Betty McCrotchart Betty Miller Betty Philips	
	William Crawford Esq. Doonside	Nancy McClatchie	
	Miss Hutchison Monkwood	Jean Phillip	
	Doctr. Logan Maybole	Janet McGavin	
	Colonel Hunter Newark*	Mrs Donaldson Jean Donald	
	Mr McMillan	Elizabeth Crawford	
	Miss Adair in Balony	unnamed	
	Miss Chalmers	unnamed	
	William Bone Innkeeper	Jean Eaglesom	
	Robert Kennedy Esq. Daljarrock	unnamed	
	Miss Kennedy	unnamed	
	Gilbert Gowdie*	Katherine Stewart	
	Hugh McHutchison Mercht.	unnamed	
	Miss Crawford	unnamed	
	Mr John Niven Mercht.	unnamed	

Parish	Master & Mistress Names & Designations	Servants' Names	Quality
	Bailie Alexander	Margaret Girvan	
	John Binning Esq.	Margaret	
	Machrimore	Montgomery	
	John McMicken Esq.	unnamed	
Dailly	Sir Andrew Cathcart of	Jean Hay	
	Carleton Bt.*	Nelly McMicken	
	John Hamilton Esq. Bargany	Mrs Buchanan	
		Barbara Hair	
		Sarah Poe	
		Janet McKenzie	
		Euphans McGechnie	
	Mr McIlwraith Senior	Elizabeth Cronnell	
	Brunston	Grizzell McCronnell	
	Sir Adam Fergusson of	Margaret Kennedy	
	Kilkerran Bt.*	Martha McClorg	
	Capt. Kennedy Drummellan	Mary Forsyth	
Straiton	John McAdam Esq.	Agnes McBride	
	Craigengillan	Nelly Blair	
		Mary Edgaret	
		Margaret Wyllie	
	James McHarg Glenfairn*	Margaret McEwan	
	David McAdam of Bennan	Mary Dobbie	
Ballantrae	Capt. Kennedy of Bennan	Elizabeth Drennan	
Barr	David Kennedy Martin of	unnamed	
	Bellimore Esq.*		
	W. Young Minister	Ann Guthrie	
Old Cumnock	Hugh Logan Esq. of Logan*	Janet Murray	
	Earl of Dumfries	Agnes Wilson	
		Agnes Murray	
		Mary Hamilton	
Auchinleck	James Boswell Esq.	Isobel Bruce	
	Auchinleck	Margaret Wallace	
	Mr Dow Minister	Isobel McKirroll	
Ochiltree	Adam Crawford Newall Esq.	Jean Graham	
	Polquhairn		
Coylton	John Steele Gadgirth	unnamed	
		unnamed	
	John Hamilton Esq. Sundrum	Mrs Smith	
		Jean Garland	
	Mr David Shaw Minister	unnamed	
Stair	Mungo Smith Esq. Drongan	Mary Reid	

Index

A

Aberdeen, Countess of............................6
Adams, Jenny 28
Adams, Samuel.....................................67
Adams, Sarah 67
Ailsa Muniments . 27, 45, 48, 71, 72, 109
Ailsa, Marquis of...........................33, 67
Aird, Jean 104
Aiton, William..
    29, 30, 34, 45, 46, 47, 52, 53, 57, 58,
    71, 102, 109
Albion (female friendly society)..........90
Alexander, Hugh 62
Allison, Robert 97
Alloway Street, Ayr............. 41, 113, 114
Anderson, Jane 29, 49
Anderson, John.....................................55
Anderson, Robert 62, 63
Annals of the Parish 57, 71
Antrim 34
Ardlochan..96
Aringa, Australia 84
arles..35
Army and Navy Co–operative Society,
    The..69
Arran 98
Auchincruive 67, 110
Auchinleck 58, 65, 72, 76, 87, 88
Auchinleck House 64
Auchinleck, Lord.................................64
Auld, Rev. William 88
Australia 79, 84
Ayr ....
    5, 12, 13, 15, 16, 24, 26, 29, 30, 31,
    34, 35, 39, 40, 41, 42, 44, 45, 46, 47,
    48, 49, 50, 54, 56, 58, 59, 64, 69, 71,
    72, 75, 77, 78, 79, 80, 83, 84, 85, 86,
    88, 89, 92, 97, 98, 99, 100, 101, 103,
    106, 107, 108, 109, 114, 115, 116,
    118, 119
Ayr Academy 105
Ayr Bank (Douglas, Heron & Co.)......85
Ayr Burgh Records 89, 107
Ayr Gold Cup.......................................35
Ayr in the Olden Times.......................60
Ayr Poorhouse 92
Ayr Savings Bank 86, 91
Ayr Welfare Home...........................30, 46
Ayrshire Archives ....
    ....5, 37, 38, 39, 65, 72, 108, 109
Ayrshire Embroidery............................75

B

Baird, James............................... 104, 105
Baird, Mrs 40
Baird, William................................ 13, 19
Ballantrae ...32, 58, 73, 74, 77, 81, 83, 92
Ballantyne, Rev. Ninian 87
Baltic..83
Balwhidder, Rev. Micah 57
Bank of Scotland.................................85
Bannerman, Mr. 81
Barcullie, by Crosshill.........................74
Bargany...
    23, 24, 25, 40, 44, 45, 66, 67, 68, 72,
    85, 102, 103, 104, 105
Barr 24, 30, 32, 49, 58, 73, 78, 87
Barr Savings Bank................................87
Barskimming.................................. 16, 17
Begbie, Alison (or Ellison)................104
Beith...60
Bell of Arnsow, Captain......................24
Bell, George Joseph 11
Bell, John 23, 44, 104
Beltane 102
Benevolent Love (female friendly
    society)..90

Berwickshire 28
Bettie, Aunt 98
Biggar, Matthew 29, 96
Blairquhan 85
Bogwood 42
Boswell, James 64
Bourtreehill 77
Boyd, William 104
Boyle, William 104
Brown, Captain, Shipmaster in Liverpool
.... 99
Brown, Elizabeth 96
Brown, John 62
Brown, Samuel 20, 95
Bruce, Janet 68
Buccleuch 68
Burnie, Thomas 85
Burns, Rev. Thomas 79
Burns, Robert ....
    16, 19, 33, 62, 63, 72, 76, 79, 81, 101,
    104
Burns, William 62
Bute, Marquess of 56, 87

C

Cadbury, Mrs 30
Caldwell 56, 71, 109
Caledonian (female friendly society) .. 90
Campbell, Captain 81
Campbell, Margaret 76
Campbell, Thomas 95
Canada 77, 78
Canada, United Provinces of 78
Cape Mounted Riflemen 79
Carbiestion 81
Carnell 104
Carnochan, David 105
Carnochan, John 96, 105
Carrick ....
    6, 31, 46, 73, 79, 81, 106, 108, 112,
    114

Carrick, Hearth Tax 73
Carruthers, Agnes 68
Cathcart Street, Ayr 41, 113
Cathcart, Gabriel 77
Cathcart, Lady 54, 55
Catrine 48, 75, 83
Catrine Cotton Mill 75, 88, 90
Chaleur, North America 78
Chancellor, Elizabeth 74
cholera 83
Church of England 24
Clark, Mrs James 41
Clyde, River 77
Colmonell 32, 58, 73, 74, 92
Committee of Emigration 78
Complete Servant, The 67, 72
consumption 56, 84
Corner, Mrs 40
Corraith 97
Correction House 12
Cottar's Saturday Night, The 67
Country Registry 41, 114
County Buildings, Ayr 5, 100
County Jail, Ayr 100
Cowan, Hugh 86
Cowan, Professor E. J. 78
Cowan, William 86
Cowan's Bank, Ayr 86
Coylton 58, 82
Craigangillan 13
Craigoch 62
Craufurd, Earl of 23, 44, 45
Crawfurd, Countess of 89
Criminal Offenders (Scotland) Report,
    1846 100
Crosbie, Mary (Mailly) 102
Crosby, William 104
Culzean ....
    15, 16, 29, 48, 53, 57, 60, 61, 62, 63,
    64, 67, 104, 110

Cumnock ....
　5, 15, 33, 34, 46, 48, 66, 81, 83, 88,
　90, 92, 99, 103, 108, 109
Cumnock Savings Bank 87
Currie, W. C. 42
Cuthill, Rev. Alexander.......................86

D

Dailly...
　13, 14, 19, 26, 27, 58, 61, 62, 72, 78,
　84, 87, 95, 98, 106, 108, 109
Daillylung...60
Dall, Mary 57
Dalmellington...................58, 76, 83, 93
Dalmellington Savings Bank..............88
Dalrymple............. 58, 74, 81, 83, 88, 90
Dalwhirr 95
Dankeith 25, 103
Davidson, Betty................................101
Devine, Professor T.M. 6, 79
Dispensary, Wallacetown 84
Disruption, the...................................79
Dixon, Jane..74
Dodds, Thomas...................................20
Domestic Servant Registries..............40
Douglas, William...............................64
Down...34
Drongan...15
druggett 61
Drummond, Robert.............................42
Dumfries................................5, 6, 63, 68
Dumfries House......... 43, 56, 66, 67, 110
Dumfries, Earl of..............................110
Dumfriesshire 14
Duncan, Rev. Dr.................................86
Dundonald 58, 79, 82, 87, 97, 98, 108
Dunlop, Catherine 94
Dunlop, David 97

E

Easton, Betty 61

Edinburgh...
　7, 16, 23, 24, 26, 27, 28, 36, 40, 44,
　45, 46, 64, 65, 68, 71, 72, 80, 106,
　107, 108, 109
Eglinton, 12th Earl of.........................76
elder (Sambucus)................................82
Ellisland 62
Employment Exchange 35
Erddig, Wales.....................................66
Erskine of Carnock, John 11, 26
Established Church 22

F

Female Emigrant's Guide and
　Companion, The..............................78
Ferguson, James 19
Ferguson, Mrs 59
Ferguson, Peggy.................................62
Fever Hospital, Ayr............................84
Findlay, Margaret...............................68
Finlayson, Malcolm............................31
flowerers 75
forgery...85
Frazer, Peter 94
Free Church................ 20, 21, 22, 27, 33
Friendly Societies........................88, 117
Frock, Captain....................................24
Fullerton, Irvine 74
Fulton, Robert 97

G

Gait, Thomas......................................68
Galloway 26, 68, 78
Galt, John 22, 71
Garden Street, Newton–upon–Ayr 98
Garven, Mrs 31
Geddies, Ann......................................62
Gemmel, Betty 62
General Assembly . 19, 21, 27, 53, 71, 99
Gibb, Mr...45
Gibson, James 99

Gillespie, James 74
Girvan ....
    5, 30, 31, 32, 49, 73, 74, 79, 81, 83,
    88, 90, 95, 97, 100, 109
Girvan Fair......................... 31
Glasgow ....
    5, 6, 25, 26, 27, 29, 45, 46, 56, 66, 70,
    71, 75, 79, 107, 109
Glasgow School of Cookery and
    Domestic Economy..................... 105
Glasgow, Past and Present 68
Glencairn, Earl of............................... 45
Glendale............................... 34
Glenton 62
Gorbals................................. 25
Gordon, Jane....................... 64
Gordon, Mr, Surveyor and acting
    Comptroller of Customs at Ayr....... 97
Goudie, Miss J 41
Goudie's Registry 41, 114
Graham, Henry.................................... 56
Graham, Margaret.................... 94
Gray, James........................... 97
Gray, James T. 33
Greenvale............................. 74
Guinea.. 15, 118

H

Hallowe'en....................................... 102
Hamilton of Bourtreehill and Rozelle,
    Robert................................ 77
Hamilton, Archibald 55
Hamilton, John.....12, 15, 24, 44, 67, 103
Hamilton, Lady Anne................. 23, 103
Handley, James 75
Hardy, Thomas................... 34
harn................................ 60
Harris, Robert................... 85
Harris, William 85
Harvest Fair.................................... 33
harvest home 102

Hearth Tax 73, 79
Hen Wife of Castle Grant, The........... 66
Hew MacKissock and Co. 78
Highland Mary 76
Highlanders, indolent 29
Hin–hairst Fair...................... 33
hiring fairs 28, 34, 36
HMS Berwick................... 74
Hogg, Hugh 60
Horn, Pamela 6
Hornbook, Dr.......................... 81
horse racing 103
House of Seclusion 83
*House with the Green Shutters, The*44,
    46
Houston, R. A. 104
Howie, Margaret................... 85
Hume, Mr 44, 45
Hume, Mrs..........25, 26, 40, 59, 68, 105
Hunter, David 97
Hunter's Bank.................... 86
Hunters (Registry etc.).........40, 114, 118

I

Inventory, The.............................. 16, 27
Irish Tattie–Howkers 29
Irishmen, vagrant............................... 29
Irvine 24, 34, 109
Irvine Savings Bank........................... 87
Isle of Man.................... 96

J

Jack's Registry 42
Jackson, Debbie................... 67
Jamieson, John.................... 85
Jamieson, Old Mill of 96
Jobbry, Archibald 22
Joppa.. 15
jupp...................................... 61
Justices of the Peace 11, 14, 47, 98

K

Kaithness, David 12
Kennedy of Kirkmichael 28, 65
Kennedy, Rankin 62
Kennedy, Scipio 15
Kennedy, Thomas Francis 78
Kennedy, William 19
Kerr, Christine...................................99
Kilbirnie 23
Kilkerran 85
Killoch.......................................85, 114
Kilmarnock.... 5, 34, 46, 62, 79, 109, 112
king's evil..84
Kirk Port, Ayr.........................40, 86, 113
Kirkbrae, Girvan................................74
Kirkdandy Fair 30, 31
Kirk–Dominae....................................30
Kirkland...74
Kirkmichael.......................................
    24, 27, 28, 42, 45, 61, 62, 65, 67, 72,
    74, 88, 104
Kirkmichael Lodge.............................42
Kirkoswald ....
    20, 27, 29, 32, 45, 48, 60, 62, 71, 72,
    74, 83, 95, 96, 98, 106, 108
kirn 102
Kyle Street, Ayr.........................41, 114
Kyle Union Poorhouse 92, 95

L

Lawson, Rev. Roderick 31, 90
Leigh Drumdow 96
Limont, Janet...................................105
Loans...97
Loch Ryan 74
Lochhead, Marion 6
Lochinch..68
Locke, Mr...102
Logan, William.......................12, 29, 64
Love and Unity (female friendly society)
   90

Lumsden, Babie 60

M

M'Hutcheon, Adam.............................86
MacCrae, James 13, 19
MacDonald, John ....
    ....23, 24, 28, 44, 45, 102, 103, 104
MacKintosh, John 85
Maclauchlin, Agnes............................95
Maclauchlin, Robert...........................95
MacMillan, Marion 104
Macqueen, Osborn 78
Maidens...74
Mair, George 42
Mauchline ....
    ....34, 42, 58, 83, 85, 88, 90, 104
Mauchline Savings Bank.....................87
Maxwell, Elizabeth 99
Maxwell, Euphan 99
May Fair...33
Maybole ....
    33, 34, 46, 58, 61, 72, 74, 79, 81, 88,
    90, 92, 99, 102, 108, 109
Maybole Combination Poorhouse ....
    .... 68, 72, 74, 92, 94, 95, 108
Maybole Savings Bank........................88
McAdam, John 13, 19
McCartney, James 31
McClelland, Thomas 86
McClillan, James...............................105
McClure, Hugh 96
McCollouch, Margaret 25
McCulloch, Isobel...............................61
McFarlane, Parlan 98
McKerrow, James 16
McKinlay, Ann....................................68
McMurtrie, Elizabeth 94
McMurtrie, Janet................................24
McNeal, John 102
McNeill, Mary....................................98
Mcrother, Betty 62

McWhirter, Andrew 25

Member, The 22, 27

Miller, Mrs 55

Miller, Sir Thomas 16, 17

Miller, William 16

Minnibole (Maybole) 32

Mitchell, Rev. John 60, 61, 62, 63

Mochrie, Rev. James 73

Modern Farmers' Guide, The 56

Monkton 58, 76, 79, 80, 97

Monkton, Ontario 77

Montgomery, Hugh 76

Montgomery, Lady Jane 55

Moodie, Thomas 68

Mossgiel 16, 62

Mount Stuart, Bute 66

Muir, Gilbert 13

Muirkirk ....
    48, 58, 59, 66, 67, 76, 81, 82, 83, 89,
    109

Murdoch, Catherine 94

Murdoch, Miss 41, 113

Mure, Elizabeth 56, 71

Murray, John 110

Mutual Support 89

N

needlework 75, 80, 86

Neil, Elizabeth 24, 25

New Bridge Street, Ayr ....
    .... 40, 42, 113, 114

New Cumnock 73

New Road North, Ayr 41

New Road, Ayr 41, 113

Newmarket Street, Ayr 40, 42, 114

Newton–upon-Ayr 114

Newton–upon–Ayr ....
    41, 58, 69, 72, 76, 84, 85, 86, 89, 98,
    103, 114

Nimmo, Robert 61

Niven, Margaret 20

Niven, Robert 62

Norman, David 42

Norman, Joseph 42

North America 76, 78

North Carolina 77

O

O'Dowd, Anne 29, 30, 34

Ochiltree 75, 88, 102

Ontario 77

Orr, David 102

Oswald, Lady Lilias 89

Oswald, Richard Alexander 86

Otago, New Zealand 79

P

Parliamentary Report on agriculture,
    1870 35

Pastoral Address 20, 22, 71

Pat's Corner, Maybole 74

Pebbles, Tibby 61

Penkill 104, 112

Penny Savings Bank 90

Penny Wedding, The 67

Pettigrew, Robert 102

Philanthropic (female friendly society) ...
    90

plague 82

Plant, Marjorie 6, 68

Poison, Daniel 104

Poor Law 18, 49, 58, 91

Poor Law (Scotland) Amendment Act
    1845 92

Poor Law Report 1844, appendix 89

Poorhouse 68, 92, 94, 95

Portpatrick 29, 68, 75, 94, 98

Post Office Savings Bank 88

Presbytery of Ayr 14, 74

Prestwick ....
    ... 15, 58, 76, 79, 80, 97, 100, 108, 114

Primrose, Dr 24

Provost, Agnes 29
Purcell, Peter 68
Purves, Sir Alexander..........................28

Q

Quebec...77
Queen's Rooms, Ayr 105

R

Race Fair 33
Redburn...74
Reform Act..17
Reform Bill..22
Reid, Mathew 97
Renfrewshire 56
Report on the Employment of Children,
   Young Persons & Women in
   Agriculture, 1867 53
Report on the Increase of Immorality in
   the Rural Districts..............................53
Ribison, Betty......................................49
Riccartoun 25
Ritchie, Archibald 20, 96
Ritchie, John..84
Robertson, Dr. David...........................81
Robertson, Francis...............................74
Robertson, Margaret............................94
Robinson, Mrs Charlotte 85
Roman Catholics 14
Ronaldson, Margaret 84
Ross, Andrew 96
Ross, Elizabeth..................................105
Ross, James 104
rowan (Sorbus)....................................82
Royal Commission on Agriculture ....
....36, 105
Royal Commission on Labour, 1893–94
....51
Royal Commission Report on Labour,
   1893 54

Rozelle ....
   23, 36, 37, 38, 39, 43, 54, 55, 71, 77,
   102, 110

S

St. Quivox 48, 58, 85, 89, 114
Sanderson, Elizabeth C. 68
Sandgate, Ayr..
   ....40, 41, 42, 69, 100, 101, 113, 114
Schullochmiln 97
Scots Herbal, The 82, 106
Scott, James.................. 40, 45, 113, 114
Scott's Registry 40, 114
Scottish Women's Rural Institute........ 63
scrofula... 84
Scythe Fair 33
Servant tax 15
Sharp, Mrs.. 40
Ship Inn, Girvan 73
Shirra 98
Shorter Catechism 19, 105
Shows, The.. 35
Skeldon 81
slaves... 15, 77
smallpox....................................... 82, 83
Smith Street, Ayr....................... 41, 114
Smith, John 85
Smith, Mungo 15
Smithy Brae, Maybole 74
Smout, T. C. 60
Smuggling................................... 95, 108
Social and Humane (female friendly
   society).. 90
Sorn................ 48, 58, 73, 76, 83, 88, 90
Sphagnum moss 82
Sprent, Mrs... 40
Stair................................ 16, 26, 58, 73
Stair House.. 102
Stair, Lord 25
Stair, Viscount.................................... 11
Stevenson, Rev. James 86

Stewart, Catherine............................ 102
stool of repentance 52
Storie, Janet.. 78
Storie, Mary 78
Story, Janet.. 25
Strachan, William 97
Straiton.............19, 25, 49, 58, 63, 88, 97
Stranraer........................... 32, 56, 74, 92
Strawhorn, Dr. John ....
.30, 46, 71, 73, 79, 106, 107, 108, 109
Stumpy Tower, Girvan...................... 100
Sundrum....................................... 12, 15
Symington..
.......25, 29, 45, 58, 62, 64, 83, 97, 103

T

Tarbolton..
.........75, 81, 84, 88, 89, 102, 106, 109
Tasmania.. 79
Thomson, Amelia.............................. 105
Tileworks, Mr. Millan's..................... 74
Tolbooth of Ayr 12, 98, 100
Trail, Betty... 16
Trail, Mrs. C. P. 78
Tremenheere, Mr............................... 105
troggers 68
Troon 58, 78, 87, 97, 106
Truck Acts... 16
tuberculosis 84

Turnberry.. 20
typhus 84

U

Union Bank.. 86
Unity Female (female friendly society)
.... 90

V

vails 23, 44
Vallance, James 97
Virginia... 77

W

Wallacetown 48, 69, 72, 83, 84, 114
Walls, Mr... 102
Warrick, Rev John 33
Webster, Peggy 61
Wellington Square, Ayr 98, 100
West Church, Maybole 90
West Indies 15, 76
whirrey, the King's 20, 96
whitework 41, 75, 101
Wilkie, Sir David 67
Willowston 97
Wilson, John 48, 81
Wood, Jean 99
Wright, James 94
Wright, Janet..................................... 94

Notes

Notes

PUBLICATIONS of the AYRSHIRE ARCHÆOLOGICAL & NATURAL HISTORY SOCIETY
available from Ronald W. Brash MA, Publications Distribution Manager
10 Robsland Avenue, Ayr KA7 2RW

Digging Up Old Ayr (Lindsay)	£1.00
George Lokert of Ayr (Broadlie)	£1.25
A Scottish Renaissance Household (MacKenzie)	£3.00
Plant Life in Ayrshire (Kirkwood/Foulds)	£4.20
The Barony of Alloway (Hendry)	£3.60
Robert Adam in Ayrshire (Sanderson)	£3.60
The Cumnock Pottery (Quail)	£5.00
Tolls and Tacksmen (McClure)	£3.60
Smuggling and the Ayrshire Economic Boom (Cullen)	£4.00
The Port of Ayr 1727–1780 (Graham)	£4.20
John Smith of Dalry, Part 1: Geology (ed. Reid)	£6.00
John Smith of Dalry, Part 2: Archæology & Natural History (ed. Reid)	£7.20
Mauchline Memories of Robert Burns (ed. Strawhorn) (reprint)	£3.50
Antiquities of Ayrshire (Grose, ed. Strawhorn) (reprint)	£4.20
Cessnock: An Ayrshire Estate in the Age of Improvement (Mair)	£4.50
Robert Reid Cunninghame of Seabank House (Graham)	£3.60
Historic Ayr: A Guide for Visitors	£2.00
A Community Rent Asunder:	£3.50
The Newmilns Laceweavers Strike of 1897 (Mair)	
The Rise and Fall of Mining Communities in Central Ayrshire (Wark)	£3.00
The Last Miller: The Cornmills of Ayrshire (Wilson)	£6.00
Historic Alloway, Village and Countryside: A Guide for Visitors	£2.00
The Street Names of Ayr (Close)	£5.00
Armstrong's Maps of Ayrshire (1775: reprint, 6 sheets)	£12.00